'*Happy Money* will transform your life because it's about how you feel about yourself, energy, and your own consciousness—as you shift that, money will flow.'

Kute Blackson, author of *You Are the One*

'Ken Honda is funny, real, and gives us the opportunity to transform our lives when it comes to money, abundance, and prosperity.'

Sheri Salata, author of *The Beautiful No*

'*Happy Money* is a direct path to a more joyful, peaceful, loving life. You'll learn to release all your old, broken stories and transform your experience of money so it can be like an old friend who is always welcome in your heart.'

Janet Bray Attwood, *New York Times* bestselling author of *The Passion Test* and *Your Hidden Riches*

'Regardless of whether you have a lot of money, some money, or not much money at all, this book will radically change your relationship with money for the better. Ken Honda is a wise and good-humored sage possessing great generosity of spirit. He is also a multi-millionaire because he lives what he teaches and writes about. This book has made a wonderful difference in my life. It can do the same for you.'

Stewart Emery, author of *Success Built to Last*

'Honda coaxes readers to examine the emotions he associates with money, and in doing so, forge a new positive (and potentially lucrative) path forward.'

Booklist

Be a part of the
Happy Money movement!

The Happy Money journey is one
most easily traveled with others.

If you would like support, additional resources,
and to connect to a community of people learning how
to live with Happy Money, please join us for free at
www.happymoneymovement.com.

happy money

The Japanese Art of
Making Peace with Your Money

ken honda

JOHN
MURRAY
LEARNING

First published in the United States in 2019 by Gallery
Books, an imprint of Simon & Schuster, Inc.

First published in Great Britain by John Murray Learning in 2019
An imprint of John Murray Press
A division of Hodder & Stoughton Ltd,
An Hachette UK company

This paperback edition published in 2020

7

Paperback ISBN 9781473684157
eBook ISBN 9781473684171

Interior design by Kyle Kabel
Printed and bound in Great Britain by Clays Ltd, Elcograf S.p.A.

John Murray Press policy is to use papers that are natural, renewable
and recyclable products and made from wood grown in sustainable
forests. The logging and manufacturing processes are expected to
conform to the environmental regulations of the country of origin.

John Murray Press
Carmelite House
50 Victoria Embankment
London EC4Y 0DZ

www.johnmurraypress.co.uk

To all the people in my life who have shared their experiences with me and who showed me the beautiful things that money can achieve, as well as the ugly ways that it can affect us, this book is for you.

Contents

CONTENTS

Is Your Money Smiling?

A few years ago, I had a unique experience that became the inspiration for the concept and title of this book. A woman whom I had just met at a party asked if she could take a look at my wallet.

As shocking as this question might be to some, it isn't particularly uncommon in Japanese culture to ask to see the contents of someone's wallet. And since there were many other people in the room, I wasn't afraid she would run away with my identity—or my money. So with little hesitation, I handed her my leather wallet.

I was a little startled, however, when she immediately went for the cash and began taking out all the large bills.

"This one's okay. This one's good. This one's good too," she said quietly to herself as she assessed each bill. For a moment I thought she was searching for something in particular. *Perhaps there are special symbols or markings on the bills?* But I soon realized she wasn't looking for anything of the sort. Then she shocked me again and began sorting the bills in a way I had never seen before.

"Good job. All of your money looks good," she said as she put the newly organized money back into the wallet and handed it back to me.

"That's great news," I said, confused yet somewhat relieved to have passed her test. "But, if you don't mind me asking, what were you looking for?"

"Oh, I was checking to see whether or not your money was smiling."

She went on to explain that money can laugh or cry depending on how it was given or received. If it is given out of guilt, anger, or sadness, the money will be "crying." In contrast, if the money is given out of love, gratitude, or happiness, the money will be smiling—even laughing—because it will be imbued with the positive energy from the giver.

Money has the ability to smile or cry?

Money changes when it is given with a certain energy or feeling?

WHAT?

Even though I was already financially well-off at the time and thought I knew much about money, I was taken aback by these insights. You see, I had always been very fortunate with money. At the age of twenty, I made a choice to be happy and wealthy by the age of thirty. So I started my own consulting and accounting business, and during my twenties I helped many people with their financial and business needs.

In the process, I did all right—in fact, well enough that at the age of twenty-nine, when my wife and I had just welcomed a newborn baby girl into our lives, I had the freedom to decide to stay home and raise her. Those were some of the happiest days of my life—and it was the best decision I ever made. Not just because I was able to spend as much time with my daughter as possible, but also because it was with her that I discovered my second career: helping *millions* of others lead happy, prosperous, and peaceful lives.

It all happened when I was at a park with my daughter on a gorgeous day. We were happily playing, when I saw a mother and her young daughter—who was about the same age as my own daughter—fighting. The mother was distressed and in a hurry. She yelled, "Your mom has to go to work! So let's go home." But the little one kept saying to her mother, "We just got here. I want to play more! Please!" After a few minutes of battle, the reluctant little girl was dragged by her mother back home. I felt so terrible for the girl and her mother. I knew that if that mother had a choice, she would have wanted to stay in the park too. After all, it was a beautiful and sunny day. What parent wouldn't want to be outside playing with their child? At that moment, I decided I needed to do something. I wanted to help not just this mother but all parents and people struggling to make ends meet. I wanted to take away her pain, stress, and frustration. So that very afternoon, after my own daughter was tired of playing, I decided I would write a short essay that would impart the wisdom I had gained over the years about making money and becoming prosperous.

When I first began, I thought I could write only five pages. But when I was finished for the day, I was amazed to see that I had written twenty-six pages in one sitting. I got so excited that I printed the essay out, stapled the pages together, and immediately started giving them away to friends. To my surprise, they loved it. Soon strangers began to call me and say they had heard about it and wanted copies of their own. So every day for several days I printed copies, stapled them together, and sent them to whoever wanted one. However, I quickly tired of stapling booklets together each day. After complaining to a friend about the process, he suggested a local printer. The salesperson on the phone talked me into ordering a 3,000 print run to cut down on costs. And, without thinking, I said okay!

Before I knew it, two trucks came to my home to drop off what looked like a warehouse full of boxes. You can imagine my wife's face when she saw the pallets of books, which filled an entire room in our house. Being the nice person she is, she forgave me. *Sort of.* She would let it slide this one time with one caveat: I had a month to get rid of all the boxes.

So what did I do? I started handing the booklets out to everyone I knew—and people I didn't. But when they were all gone, I continued to get requests and orders. At first I didn't know if people were requesting them because the content was good or because it was free. Nevertheless, I knew I was onto something. And when I reached 100,000 copies given away, I definitely knew. At that point a publisher actually called me and asked me if I would be interested in writing an entire book. My first response: "No way! I am not a writer!" But the publisher was insistent: "You have all the time in the world. Why don't you give it a try?" I couldn't argue with his point. My daughter was on her way to kindergarten soon, and then what would I do with all my time?

I guess I could write.

And that's exactly what I did.

Since that fateful day on the playground, I have published more than fifty books and sold almost eight million copies in Japan. Not bad for a retired dad who had an idea on the playground with his daughter. What began as a stroke of insight and an urge to help out a struggling working mother turned into not only a career but my purpose in life. That purpose, I realized, was to help others find *theirs*—and to become prosperous and free in the meantime. Needless to say, after writing fifty books, I thought I had this "money thing" pretty much figured out. But when my new friend, the Mysterious Wallet Woman, handed me back my wallet, I got to thinking again just as I had done all those years ago back on the playground.

This time I started to think about money as energy.

MONEY AS ENERGY

Holding the wallet my new friend had just returned to me, I thought: *What a relief. All the money I have earned over the years and received came from happy people—grateful and joyful people.* I then thought briefly about how I had earned my money. Yes, I had indeed received all my money through service. I had helped others become successful, wealthy, and empowered. I had helped others gain a sense of peace, joy, and gratitude. I thought how the people who paid me felt when they read my books or attended my seminars and workshops. (Throughout the world, I have given seminars to thousands of people at a time.) Then I thought about my books and how many people have changed their own lives because of them. They changed jobs, got married, had babies, and left unhappy or toxic relationships. I have heard from many who have started their own businesses. Some even have grown their businesses from nothing to publicly traded companies. I've also heard from others who didn't become fabulously wealthy but who felt rich—and were very happy no matter what their bank statements reported. No longer affected by money-related stress, they were free to take out a new lease on life. Although I am often called a "money guru" or "money healer," my real job over the past decade, I realized while standing there and looking at my wallet, had been to help others find the tools they already possessed *within themselves* to heal their own lives and relationships with money. Then it occurred to me that, yes, *all the people who had given me their money had infused it with these feelings of gratitude and joy—so much happy energy.* All this smiling money in my wallet was there because of others. *Of course! Of course money is energy!* Then I began thinking about my own feelings and the energy I pass along to others when I use money.

I stood there for a few seconds and I realized: *There are so many emotions wrapped up in our money!* So many of us walk around with all this energy, and it impacts not only ourselves but others as well. We like to think that money is just a number or a piece of paper, but it is so much more than that. Money brings with it so many emotions—more than we even realize. Even when we are aware of it—such as when we feel stressed about our endless stacks of bills, our meager paychecks, or our lack of savings for the future—we often think we are powerless. We feel hopeless and defeated. We even feel resentful and jealous of others who have more than us. We may even give up trying to earn more or receive more. Instead we say things like: "That's just the way it is, and there isn't much we can do about it!" So many of us think of money as the enemy, this dark force that is keeping us from living the life we're supposed to have or doing the things we love. So few of us see the potential that money has to bring us joy, gratitude, and happiness—especially when we give it away freely and with the same positive energy as we received it.

After my new friend the Mysterious Wallet Woman gave me back my money, I looked down and noticed the cash tucked safely away in the pocket. And it got me thinking: *So much money exists in the world. There is so much money out there right now spreading happiness and love. But so much is also spreading sadness and fear.*

I wondered what, if anything, I could do to help infuse the world with as much love, gratitude, joy, prosperity, and peace as possible. I wondered how I could spread around as much Happy Money as possible. And so an idea came to me, much as it had all those years ago in the park with my daughter. I would write a book. I would share these insights with others—as many people as I possibly could. And this book, *Happy Money*, is the essence of what I have taught and learned from so many others. I'll try to help you answer the questions that so many people have asked me to answer over the years:

- How can I deal with money?
- Can I have more money without incurring great sacrifice?
- Can I have peace while I am alive?
- What can I do to create a happy, fulfilling, prosperous, and purpose-filled life?

All those questions will be answered in this book. As my other books have changed millions of people's lives, this book will change yours too.

My greatest hope is that this book will help you look at your life in a totally different way and transform your relationship with money. The comment I most often get from my readers is: "Wow, this is new. I've never thought of money this way." I hope you have the same feeling. I hope it will be the start of your Happy Money life.

I guarantee it will be an exciting one.

Happy Money and Unhappy Money

There are two kinds of money: Happy Money and Unhappy Money. Happy Money is the kind that a ten-year-old boy uses to buy flowers for his mom on Mother's Day. Happy Money is when parents gladly pinch pennies in order to save a few extra dollars each week to be able to send their kids to soccer camp or take piano lessons. There are so many ways regular old money can become Happy Money:

- helping a struggling family member out of a bind
- sending a few dollars to those affected by a hurricane
- raising money by selling cookies for a homeless shelter
- investing in a business or community project
- receiving money for work or services from satisfied clients.

All the money circulated with love, care, and friendship is Happy Money. Happy Money makes people smile and feel loved and cared for deeply. It is in many ways an active form of love—a way in which people can see, feel, and touch. Often money can help others in a way that nothing else can.

For example, when someone is going through a major hardship, like losing their entire home to a fire, "thoughts and prayers" and "good vibes" will get them only so far. However, I guarantee you that money will help a family get back on their feet, buy them food, and give them a temporary roof over their heads in a way that good vibes just can't.

Conversely, Unhappy Money is the kind of money you use to begrudgingly pay your rent, bills, and taxes. We don't have to stretch our imaginations too far. We've all experienced the many forms of Unhappy Money:

- paying or receiving money as alimony after an ugly divorce
- receiving a salary from an employer for a job you don't like but can't bring yourself to leave
- unwillingly paying off credit cards with huge interest rates
- receiving money from someone who resents paying you—like an unhappy customer who says, "You don't deserve it, but I'll pay you anyway to honor the contract"
- stealing money—from anyone.

Money circulated in frustration, anger, sadness, and despair is Unhappy Money. This kind of money makes people stressed, desperate, aggravated, depressed, and sometimes violent. It deprives people of their dignity, self-esteem, and gentleness of heart. Whenever you receive and spend money and you do so with negative energy, it becomes Unhappy Money.

CHOOSING YOUR FLOW

If there are two kinds of money, then there are only two ways to deal with money. We are in a flow of either Happy Money or Unhappy Money. Depending on which flow you choose, your life and the outcomes in your life will vary.

Let me state this plainly: *It is not how much you make or have* that makes you have Happy Money or Unhappy Money; *it is the energy with which your money is given and received* that determines your flow. Whether you make a lot of money or very little, your money can be in either flow.

Ultimately, it is your choice. If you want to be in the flow of Happy Money, you can. You can choose to be grateful when you receive money and you can give generously and with joy and enthusiasm. However, based on my experience working with thousands of individuals in seminars and workshops who have come to me seeking advice about money, I realized this is easier said than done. Most people aren't mindful of their relationship to the flow of money. **In fact, I would venture to say that most people, whether they realize it or not, are already in a deeply committed, unhappy relationship with their money.**

And where there is Unhappy Money, there are unhappy people. The two go hand in hand, if you will. For example, if your family and the people immediately around you—at school, in the workplace, or in social groups—are in flow with an Unhappy Money group, chances are you've been on the receiving end of some seriously resentful, ungrateful, and joyless money.

Since most of us don't have a healthy relationship with money, we spend a lot of our precious time worrying about and resenting money. Some of us resent it and find it so difficult to comprehend that we don't even want to think about it—ever. Even if we know on some level that we'll have to deal with it at some point, we avoid it at all costs. In fact, some of us are so tired from worrying about a lack of money that we have little energy for anything else in life. We become weighed down by the burden of working, making ends meet, and keeping up with our neighbors. It becomes so overwhelming, in fact, that we let the bills stack up. We don't pay bills. We don't count the money in our wallet and we avoid looking at our bank statements. And then our problems, like interest, compound.

So few of us realize just how much energy is required to think about money or how much money determines even our most basic decisions.

I want you to stop and think about it for a moment. Do your friends and family vary widely in their financial resources and backgrounds? Do you run with a country club crowd, or are most of your friends working nine-to-five gigs? Do your friends have similar homes or cars? So many of us think it's an accident or luck that we meet or socialize with the people we do, but chances are our socio-economic status determines much in our lives—whether we like it or not.

So, yes, our life is controlled by money to some extent. Who we are, where we went to school, where we grew up, who we become friends with, who we make connections with in the working world, and how we choose to make and spend our money determine so much in our lives. And let me assure you, it is not only the poor and the middle class who are affected by the flow of money and who can receive and give money infused with negative energy. The upper-middle-class and wealthy folks are also influenced by the negative flow of money. I know plenty of wealthy clients who, though richer than Midas, are deathly afraid of losing what they have. They have no idea how to even enjoy their money: they are constantly stressed-out trying relentlessly to keep up with the Joneses.

Of course, if being rich is your goal, you can aim for that. But most people realize that making a lot of money isn't going to solve all their problems. In fact, many people realize they don't even need to have a lot of money to create their ideal lives. Rather, it's those who figure out how to change their attitude toward and their relationship with money by healing their past wounds associated with money who seem to feel the wealthiest, regardless of what they have.

SO WHAT IS MONEY?

During the last half of my career, I focused on healing the money wounds that people have. When most people realize what these wounds are, how they occurred, and how they have affected their daily lives, they start to create healthy priorities in life. If you heal the pain you have about money, your financial situations will absolutely change—and dramatically so. Your money—and hence your life—is a reflection of your beliefs about money. If you believe it is something that can be used for good, that is abundant, and that can be given and received freely, your outer life will begin to reflect that inner change. But if you hold on to negative mind-sets and false beliefs about money—that it is evil, that it creates drama, that it is the root cause of all that is bad in your life—you can bet that your outer reality will soon reflect that inner monologue.

EARLY EXPERIENCES WITH UNHAPPY MONEY

Although I never intended to become a writer who helped people with money, my quest for Happy Money started when I was very small. When I was at an early age, money had a huge impact on my life. In many ways the lessons I learned as a child have stuck with me to this day.

My father was an accountant with a successful private business. When his clients were visiting, it was my job to wait on them and serve them tea. I amused myself by finding opportunities to ask all these experienced business-men questions they'd never expect an eight-year-old boy to know anything about. Many didn't know how to react when I started inquiring about that month's sales profits, return on equity, turnout ratio, or shareholder incentives. It was a fun hobby.

At a certain point I started to notice that although some of my father's clients started off wearing somewhat shabby clothes, over time they began walking in with nice suits and expensive shoes. Many upgraded their cars while they were at it. At the same time I observed that others seemed to be moving in the opposite direction.

Even among the clients who appeared to be wealthy, eventually it became apparent to my eight-year-old self that most people could be divided into two general types: the irritated, rushed, and busy, and the peaceful, content, and happy.

One afternoon something occurred that shook me to the core and has remained with me ever since. I came home from elementary school to find my otherwise stoic father crying. This was the man who had taught me karate and kendo. He had taught me to stand up to bullies and protect people who were getting hurt. I couldn't imagine anything that would make him cry, but there he was, in stark contrast to his usual self, seemingly falling apart before my eyes.

My mother took me aside and told me that my father felt responsible for a tragedy that had occurred. One of my father's clients had murdered his entire family and then killed himself. Because my father had denied the man a loan when he had come desperately begging for money a few days earlier, he felt he was to blame.

Later I found out that although my father initially had said no, he had fully intended to lend his client the money at a later date. He wanted to help his client's family recover from their severe financial situation but wanted to prevent that money from falling directly into the pockets of loan sharks who would profit from their suffering.

With a heavy heart, my father arranged the funeral. The consequences of his actions were never far from his mind, and he fell into a period of dark depression and began abusing alcohol. He never fully recovered. His smile disappeared and so did our family's. It was devastating.

Until then I had never regarded money with anything other than positive feelings. Children do not inherently associate money with fear. For the first time I realized that money could bring you much more than just success and happiness: one mistake and you could lose your entire family. This memory formed a distinct impression on me about the dark consequences of money.

That was the day I made up my mind to be financially secure when I grew up and got married, so my own family would never suffer a similar fate.

I might have been too young to be totally conscious of it, but this event impacted my entire view of money. Even if my family was financially comfortable, what good was it if people around us were having financial difficulties? After all, we are always affected and influenced by those who are closest to us.

I decided to pursue the quest for the meaning of money. What was its purpose? A few years later I observed a phenomenon of sorts. Japan was going through what was later called a "bubble economy." Again I witnessed firsthand the relationship people had with money—what happened when they had a lot of it and then, quite suddenly, none of it.

After getting into college, I looked for great teachers who could teach me about business and money. Again I recognized a dichotomy: there were two kinds of wealthy people, the happy ones and the unhappy ones. The happy ones seemed to have great relationships with their families, and all of them worked in fields that they loved. They also received great respect from employees and clients alike, and would give the shirts off their backs to people in need. Conversely, I observed, unhappy wealthy people were thinking about how much more they could make and how to increase their net worth. All they could think about was creating new business and taking advantage of other people legally. They were your classic two-faced con artists: they tended to treat their employees poorly and were rude to waiters and drivers, but behaved well with those who could give them money or do something to help them get ahead.

What made the two so different?

I knew that there had to be a reason behind their behavior. There also had to be some kind of formula, something that added up. Why did some people who had money become happy and generous while others did not?

Little did I know that I was beginning a lifelong pursuit of Happy Money.

CHAPTER I

What Does Money Mean to You? Solving the Mystery of Money

Before I begin to explain what money is, the better question to start this chapter with is: What does money mean to *you*?

I am sure that, depending on who is asking, your answers will vary slightly. For example, if a nine-year-old girl asked you, "What is money?" you might answer her with "There are two kinds of money: paper bills and coins. You can buy stuff with money."

But what if you were explaining money to an adult? Would you say, "Money is a medium of exchange for goods and services"?

While both answers are correct, you and I know there is more to money than "a medium of exchange" or something you simply use to "buy stuff with." We make and spend money every day, yet we cannot answer this one simple question.

I have asked people for years the following question: "What does money mean to you?"

I'm always surprised by the answers I receive. After asking thousands of people from countries all over the world,

I never hear the same answer. It means something different to each person. I recall one person telling me money is a heavenly god, while another said it is the devil. I have heard money explained to me by some as an expression of love, and by others as a slave driver. The extreme diversity in answers to this question demonstrates that the meaning of money depends on the person.

On the surface, physical money is just a simple piece of paper or metal. However, even if all the people around you have the same faces printed on those pieces of paper and the same designs stamped on each coin, it's incredible how much variety there is in the meaning it holds for each of us. When looking at that coin, some people will feel anger rising up, while others will feel joy. But what's really interesting is that we don't have the same emotional reaction whatsoever, even when looking at toy money made for children—except for, perhaps, Monopoly money. Why? Because the types of emotional reactions we have when playing the game, for the most part, are fairly consistent with how we react to real money. Since we often play the game Monopoly to *win*, we approach that money with the same energy and attachment we do when we spend money in real life. Who among us doesn't want to "win"—or what we collectively think of as "winning"—in real life: earning more money, owning desirable properties, not having to pay a lot in income taxes, and avoiding going to jail? Who among us doesn't rejoice at the surprise surplus of cash or a payout of dividends when the "chance" card says we have won it—in the game of Monopoly or in real life? In other words, whatever our feelings toward property and money are in real life, we will attach those same feelings to Monopoly money. How do you feel about owning property? Paying taxes? Paying rent? Are you conservative in your purchases or do you go all out and take risks? Play the game yourself and observe yourself and others, and see what emotions bubble up with each throw of the dice. If you want to see just how much emotional energy we attach to those pieces of paper and metal coins in real life, see the energy you attach to them when you're playing a game. I promise, it will be revelatory.

In my experience, the people who have the most fun, feel the most confident, and realize it's just a game always come out ahead. They may not have the most money in the bank, but they remain unattached to the outcome of "winning" or having "the most" and enjoy the process—the give-and-take. They focus on "feeling" like a winner rather than on actually winning.

SO HOW DO YOU WANT TO PLAY THE MONEY GAME?

What if I told you, money is a *game*?

How well do you play now?

Would you consider yourself to be winning?

Once again, "winning" is not how well you do financially. It is how good you *feel about playing*.

Unlike Monopoly, in which you move around the board in a consistent manner and pretty much know what to expect, playing with your money in real life isn't so predictable. You're not moving five spaces or twelve spaces and in a clockwise direction. Most of us, in fact, feel pretty lost when we're playing the real-life money game. We don't know which property is going to yield the most returns. We don't know if the house we own is going to become infested with mold or a tree is going to fall on it. We don't know if a family member is going to get cancer, incur huge medical bills, and lose the ability to contribute to the family income for several years while they fight the illness. We don't know if the company we work for is going to make some bad financial decisions and will have to lay us off someday. We don't know if the industry we've spent our life working for will become obsolete when another, disruptive industry comes in and takes over. The truth is the game of money we're playing in real life is pretty fraught. Economic changes, family issues, and natural disasters sure have a way of making us feel lost.

In fact, most of us feel like we've lost the game before we even get to roll the proverbial dice. And we're told that things "could change" if we just work a little harder, a little smarter. So we do.

Sound familiar?

Chances are if you're reading this book, you've been told these rules of engagement already: *Work hard and the money will follow.* Let me tell you something that you already probably know on an instinctive level: people who have more money or seem wealthier than you aren't any smarter than you or working any harder than you. A lot of people in this world have worked themselves to death and never had two nickels to rub together. Let me assure you: working harder isn't the only answer. I know a lot of smart, hardworking people who don't feel they are compensated enough and aren't winning the money game. And I also know a lot of people who feel they have enough and have nothing to worry about. Interestingly, many of these folks don't have more money than my seemingly wealthy friends.

A TRICKY GAME BECAUSE RULES KEEP CHANGING

The money game is an interesting one. My mentor Wahei Takeda once said, "There is no end in the money game." It's like baseball. Even if you are winning in the bottom of the ninth inning, that doesn't guarantee a win. An exceptional hitter can bring everyone on base home with just one crack of the bat. The money game is the same. Even if you are wealthy in your thirties or forties, that doesn't mean something disastrous won't happen and leave you destitute and unable to retire in your sixties. We've all heard of people who seemed to earn enough money to last for several lifetimes but who had to file for bankruptcy. Examples abound of famous wealthy celebrities and athletes who lost everything they made and died with massive amounts of debt.

Sometimes people lose their money because they've spent way beyond their means, but other times it's because the rules of money kept changing (or what constitutes "money" changes).

Look at the real estate bubble of 2008. For years before that, people were told: "Invest in real estate. That's where the money is." Housing prices soared, and loans were easy to qualify for. But the "rules" changed. The housing market plummeted seemingly overnight. The houses that people owned—houses they were sure they could sell for double the price they paid, as they had in the past—were worth almost nothing.

People moved on to gold. "Gold is golden," financial experts say when there is turmoil in every other market. But when the economy is good, gold becomes just a yellow metal that doesn't generate any interest.

We are approaching an interesting time when all sectors of the global economy are connected more than ever but the system as we know it is falling apart. New systems are appearing every day, and even how we think of and experience money is changing. For example, these days everyone in financial circles is talking about cryptocurrency. It's "the future" and "the most reliable system." And yet there is a lot of chatter about hacking. What seems to be "the most reliable system" cannot be trusted either.

There are so many experts and financial gurus out there claiming to know where the next best place to invest your money is or how to make more money. And many of the gurus are saying the opposite thing! So what or who can you trust?

When it comes to money, what, if anything, is in your control?

I would venture to say *how we feel about money* is what we can control. And that has more to do with our feelings about being wealthy than any real estate, stock, gold, or cryptocurrency market out there.

WHAT IS MONEY, REALLY?

True, there was a time when the "form" of money used to be simpler. Just a hundred and fifty years ago, when people wanted to buy something at a market, they paid in cash. At that time, they had only bills and coins. Now we have checks, bank accounts, credit cards, Venmo, Pay-Pal, and cryptocurrency. The money we use at a grocery store and the money that travels electronically on Wall Street seems very different today from what it was in centuries past.

There was a time not too long ago when people stuck their money under mattresses or in safes in their own homes. They had to see and touch the money regularly to know that it was there and in their possession. However, money is just a symbol when you think about it. We rarely see it or touch it in its printed form today. We only need to click on our phones and see our bank statements to know that our money exists. Most of us receive money through our bank accounts and then we spend it with a credit card. It's not uncommon to go days, weeks, or months without ever needing to touch cash. In most parts of Asia, Japan in particular, people rarely carry wallets anymore because every transaction is easily taken care of with their smartphones.

Simultaneously, billions of dollars, euros, marks, and yen are being traded all over the world. We cannot perceive that the money we use every day and the money traveling around in the electronic world are the same. Today a hedge fund manager can make the equivalent of somebody's annual income in just a few minutes. These things confound us.

How is this even possible?

SO WHERE IS YOUR MONEY?

The concept of money is actually quite vague when you think about it. The money you think you have in the bank is not really there. Once you deposit your money, the banks lend it to someone else. So physically your money is no longer there. All that remains are those numbers you saw when you checked your bank account on your smartphone.

Let's try this as a thought experiment. You may think you have money, but what if it's an illusion? As scary as this idea is, suppose you check your statement one day and there is no money there. You haven't spent it. It's just gone. You call the bank and say, "Where is my money?" And the bank says, "You don't have any money in the account." How would you be able to prove otherwise? Do you have records of deposits made? Sure. Do you have transaction histories? Sure. But what if the bank says it doesn't have any of that? How do you prove the hours you worked, the interest you accrued, the amount of money you deposited?

Imagine how you would feel if it all disappeared.

Now let's think of the money you owe: college loans, credit card debt, mortgages. Maybe you feel burdened by these loans. Now, just as you imagined the money you have in your checking or savings account was an illusion of sorts, imagine that your loans and debts were illusions too. What if they all just disappeared? (We don't quite have the same angst about these types of illusions disappearing that we do when our money disappears. Go figure.)

Most of us, however, trust the system we operate in. We trust that the banks will give us our money back when we ask for it, and we trust that we owe the amounts of our loans and that we have to pay them. We feel safe that our money is in the bank, and we feel stressed that we have loans to pay off.

Now that we seem to know where our money is, we have to ask ourselves: What is it for, really? And where does it all seem to go?

WHERE DOES ALL YOUR MONEY GO?

All our lives, we study, work hard, and pay taxes. But after paying all the bills, most of us have very little at the end of each month. We have college loans, car loans, credit card debt, and mortgages, all of which feels like an enormous burden, with no relief in sight. And then, as if to add insult to injury, compared to our income there is never enough for us to spend on what we are "supposed" to have. We are bombarded with advertising at every turn for these supposedly must-have items. We need the newest model of the luxury car we just bought. The "old" SUV won't do anymore. We need upgrades to our phones. We have friends who have traveled to exotic locations or taken their families to Disney World—not once but every year—and we feel like we're missing out if we don't make the trip ourselves. There is even a term now for this: "FOMO"—*fear of missing out*. Everyone has a case of FOMO these days. Whether it's cosmetic cream or a dress or suit that will make us more handsome, more beautiful, or richer looking, we just *have* to buy it or we're missing out. The list is endless: new home improvements, new gadgets, new shoes, new experiences. It's all *new, new, new*, all the time. We are constantly told by advertisers, television shows, and even our friends that what we have isn't good enough anymore. True, we are not going to die if we don't have any of these things, but our kids just might. What parent hasn't heard "I'll just die if I don't have what my friend [insert name] has"? Or: "Everyone *but me* has [insert whatever is the latest fashion or gadget trend] and I'll look like a loser if I don't have it! Please, Mom and Dad, can I have it?" And kids aren't the only ones who do this. We all know someone who is always bragging about their latest purchase, and then we go back to our own homes and think to ourselves, *Well, this television—which I loved up until an hour ago—is cheap and outdated. I need a new one too!*

And when we can't afford those things that our friends have, we get confused and upset. We see people of privilege enjoying life without doing anything (or so we tell ourselves), and we get angry. "I work just as hard if not harder! I deserve good things too," we complain. We tell ourselves we are doing everything right—but we still don't have enough. *It's never enough.* Someone always has something better. Someone is always doing more. Something is not right.

"It's just not fair," we say.

When my daughter was young, I moved my family to Boston for a year for my daughter's education. At the time she didn't speak much English and came home one day and asked me about a phrase she kept hearing throughout the day. She said, "Daddy, everyone said this one sentence and I want to know what it means." I asked her what it was. She then told me the sentence kids were using all day was "It's not fair!"

I couldn't help but smile.

Yes, when it comes to money and life, all over the world we feel and hear "It's not fair!" on a regular basis. Children hear their parents say it at home. "It's not fair that so-and-so makes more than me! It's not fair how hard I work and how little I get paid for my efforts!" And then our kids go to school and see a child playing with a doll they desire and they say, "It's not fair that she has that doll right now and I don't!" Or: "It's not fair that he gets to be on the swing for all of recess and I don't!" And a teacher may have to be called in and explain to the children: "There is enough time for everyone to ride on the swings; just wait your turn." Or: "There are plenty of other toys to play with; let's go find you one." The teacher is correct: there is enough time and there are enough swings, dolls, toys, etc., but children cannot see that. They see only what they *don't have*, what they *aren't doing*—just as their parents are seeing only what they don't have and what they aren't doing. This is what we call the myth of scarcity.

THE MYTH OF SCARCITY

People everywhere in the world feel they are not treated fairly. Many of us believe that it's a zero-sum game. If someone else has something, then we can't have it. We believe that if others have a lot of money, they are automatically depriving us of our money. We attach a lot of negative emotions to money when we think of it this way. The scarcity mind-set is a belief that there are limited resources in the world and if we don't get what we want when we want it, someone else will. We have to get it soon, because it's running out. And if it's running out, we have to do everything in our power to make sure we have it before anyone else does. All sorts of negative influences drive our behavior when we think like this. We operate out of fear, jealousy, and greed. We take what we can get, whenever we can get it, and we don't think about how it affects others or the greater good. But this way of thinking never serves us for very long. Because when we do get what we want, it's still never enough. Because there is always going to be something bigger, better, and more desirable out there, and if we don't have that either, we'll be missing out. It's an endless cycle that keeps us trapped in a never-ending process of accumulation and spending and then wanting more. One of the greatest books about the scarcity mind-set and its devastating consequences is *The Soul of Money: Transforming Your Relationship with Money and Life* by my friend Lynne Twist, a global activist and founder of the Pachamama Alliance. Lynne is recognized throughout the world for her insights and her achievements in helping to alleviate global hunger, ensure women's rights, and inspire people to live lives of integrity, generosity of spirit, and abundance. She writes: "This internal condition of scarcity, this mind-set of scarcity, lives at the very heart of our jealousies, our greed, our prejudice, and our arguments with life." Every argument, every prejudice, every petty disagreement comes down to the idea that someone is getting something I am not—which is at the heart of scarcity. Therefore, to overcome jealousy, fear, greed, and prejudice, we must eliminate the idea of scarcity—the idea that things just aren't "fair."

The reason my daughter was hearing "It's not fair" all day was that, in every instance, the children were looking at what they didn't have and not what they did. I imagine the child who wanted the doll finally did get the doll. And I have no doubt that while that child was playing with the doll, another child had not only a doll but also a carriage for the doll! *Well, that's just not fair.*

And the same goes for us adults. We have a house. We have a car. We have clothes. But our neighbors have more expensive clothes with fashionable labels on them, bigger homes, and more expensive and flashier cars. *They are wealthy. They have more. And if they have more, then I have no chance at getting it. They've taken my piece of the pie.*

But have they? Let's look at this a little more in depth.

LOSING OUR PEACE OF MIND BECAUSE OF MONEY

How many dreams and marriages have been torn apart because of money?

How much peace of mind have we lost?

More than we should.

When I ask a roomful of people about stressful childhood experiences related to money, I inevitably hear something along the lines of "I wanted to take ballet classes, but my mom told me we couldn't afford it." Substitute ballet with baseball, gymnastics, ice-skating, or any number of hobbies we dreamed of pursuing as children, and it's safe to say we have all heard that story in one form or another.

As counterintuitive as this sounds, those among us whose parents told us directly that we were too poor when we were young should consider ourselves lucky. Sure, we may now feel resentment toward money, but at least we don't continue to blame ourselves for our parents' money troubles. Some unfortunate children suffer needlessly and feel like it's their fault their parents are poor. Their parents constantly complain about how much it costs to provide for them; some even go so far as to say, "I would be rich if it weren't for you kids." And then there are parents who operate in a more passive-aggressive, damaging way. Out of embarrassment or anger over their financial circumstances, these parents tell their kids that the reason they can't take those hockey lessons is because they never follow through on anything—or, worse, they aren't talented enough and it would be a waste of money. And what does a child think when he or she hears that? *I'm a waste of money.* This painful distortion of the truth is more likely the unintentional result of the parents' psychological issues than an attempt at manipulation, but the end result is the same: the children of these parents come to associate money with pain and suffering—and they internalize it so much that they believe they are the *root cause* of the suffering. Talk about emotional baggage!

ROOTING THROUGH OUR EMOTIONAL GARBAGE RELATED TO MONEY

Does money help you with whatever you want to do?

Or is it an obstacle that always gets in your way?

Because of money, have you been unable to start your dream project or leave your unsatisfying job?

Do you like money?

Does money like you too?

What stories do you tell yourself about money?

Do you find yourself saying the same things your parents did about money? *(There's never enough. I wish I had more. I work so hard and still don't earn enough.)*

Money, as we said earlier, comes in various forms, but it is simply an object in its simplest state. Yet we project so many feelings onto money. I actually feel a little sorry for money, because it is an easy target of resentment and jealousy and always gets blamed for all the wrongdoings of humankind.

But it's not money that's the problem. *We're* the problem.

For some people, money means security. For others, money is a monster that can rip them apart at any moment. For still others it is a symbol of freedom—or it represents the control exerted over them by their boss or parents or family.

By checking whatever feeling you project onto money, you can recognize your own emotional baggage. If you can do that, you can see money clearly.

Why is this so difficult? Because getting to that place takes a lot of understanding and introspection. It means digging deep and figuring out what your own beliefs about money are, understanding how you developed these beliefs, and ultimately discovering what money means to you.

THREE FUNCTIONS OF MONEY

Confusion about what money is and what it means to us is often closely linked to a feeling. We may feel used, discarded, or taken advantage of. We feel like life is unfair. We feel unworthy and diminished. We feel that others have more than we do. A lot of these feelings result from the functions of money. Money primarily serves three functions:

The Function of Exchange

Most people can relate to this. We use money in exchange for something. It can be food, a train ticket, or an hour of massage therapy. This exchange function gives money power, because once we obtain money, we feel like we can exchange it for anything. It is almost an automatic process or an innate desire. Since we inherently need things to survive—food, clothing, shelter—we need a means to obtain those things: money. When we don't have enough money to do so, we panic. We feel like our lives or our families' lives are in peril, and everything related to money—earning and spending money—becomes stressful.

The Function of Saving

Another reason people want to hold on to their money is that they want to preserve its value and, by extension, their own value. For example, in the Stone Age, humans hunted giant mammoths. If they didn't eat an entire mammoth immediately or figure out a way to store it or make use of its parts, it would decay, and the work and effort of months of tracking the beast would be wasted. In order to preserve the value of their work and effort, they had to save, use, or trade the meat. The same goes for us. We don't want our labor to be in vain. We want it to retain its value. We want to see money in the bank after a hard workweek. We want to see savings accrue after years of dedicated service.

In other words, we want to have something to show for our life's work. We want it to mean something. When we work week after week, year after year, and have nothing to show for it, we become dejected and depressed and feel like our lives lack meaning. We equate one's life's worth with his net worth.

The Function of Growth

This is the core of capitalism. If you deposit money, it generates interest. So if you have money invested, it grows like a living thing. People who have more money get more money. This is why the wealthy get wealthier. Most of us are confused by this concept, because it means that hard work and effort have little to do with one's success. We can also feel excluded. If we don't have any money left over to invest at the end of each month after paying our bills, how on earth will we ever generate enough money to accrue wealth?

It's easy to see why the functions of money can make us feel inadequate or like the deck is stacked against us before we even begin to play the card game. But even if that feels true, it doesn't stop us from trying to make more money or *wanting it*.

So if money is such trouble, why do we also seem to want more money in the first place?

SIX REASONS PEOPLE WANT MONEY

Everyone wants more money. When you randomly ask a person what they want most, they will often reply, "Money." They can decide exactly how to use it later.

Why do we want money so much? What are the underlying motivations that keep us constantly feeling in need of money? Once you can put into perspective the emotional reasons for wanting money, you will start to feel more connected to your own needs and less stressed about money. This is how you can be released from money's control over you.

Over the years I've observed many reasons why people think they want money. I've recognized some distinct patterns, which I am going to describe as the six reasons why people want money.

There is always an emotional drive behind wanting money. But if we become disconnected from the underlying emotions, we can get stuck in a cycle of trying to make money without understanding what we really need.

Reason #1: To Maintain a Basic Standard of Living

We all need shelter, clothes, and food to eat—and a way to cook it. In the past, people attributed their livelihood to good farmland and forest, but today it is money that delivers to us the things we need. When most people are asked why they are working, they will reply, "To put food on the table." It is important to understand the difference between what we consider to be the bare minimum and what we consider luxury.

I've met many people who were making good salaries yet constantly felt like they had just enough to put food on the table and keep a roof over their heads. When I looked at how they were spending their money, they had a house at the highest limit of their price range and a new car with an expensive lease, and spent a huge percentage of their monthly income on food and entertainment. They also often had a home full of things they didn't actually use. The problem is that people connect money directly to survival, so whenever they feel like they have a need, their instinct is to turn to money and buy something.

Reason #2: To Gain Power

Money is often seen as something that has the power to control people and make them do things. So it is not surprising that we regard rich people as powerful.

But being powerful does not mean that you are in control, nor does it mean happiness. When we confuse money and power in this way, we never satisfy our need to feel in control of our own lives and are left always wanting more power, and thus more money. And just like there is always someone with more money, there is always someone with more power. This corruptive and addictive force brings all kinds of negative emotions that block true happiness from our lives.

Sometimes I meet very ambitious young people, and they say things to me about how they want to build a business empire and become one of the wealthiest people in the world. But what they don't understand is that even though wealth brings some power, money is not a replacement for things like integrity and trust and genuine love. You will never be able to win the hearts of people with money alone. I have come across many people who are powerful in business and society but who feel powerless in their close relationships and in their own state of mind.

Reason #3: To Get Back at Others

All kinds of people, rich or poor, feel abused by others at times. If they are poor, they feel robbed of certain privileges; if they are rich, they feel disrespected or excluded by their peers. People who feel slighted by society can then be tempted to see money as a way to get revenge on those who held them back or made them suffer.

But the bullies are just in their minds. The person who is really judging them is themselves. And yet they will buy things to compete with others, not realizing that no one is really competing against them. Even people who can't afford very expensive things can get wrapped up in using material items to puff themselves up as superior to others, just on a smaller scale.

Some self-made millionaires try to show off their wealth as a way to compensate for other insecurities, but no matter how much they make or spend, their self-esteem never improves. They constantly feel that others are looking down on them or talking about them behind their backs.

Reason #4: To Find Freedom

Some people think that money can buy freedom. When we think of freedom, we usually imagine a life without a job and with the ability to go anywhere in the world and do anything we want. And to live freely like that, you have to have tons of money.

But freedom can't be bought with money. Even if you have all the money in the world, if your mind is not free, you lose the real advantages of that wealth. Unless you are able to find freedom in the present moment, you will always come back to the same emotional states even after you win the lottery or get a huge inheritance. Money can buy things that will make you feel happy temporarily, but without true fulfillment that comes from within, true freedom will escape you.

The truth is that many of us have more freedom and more options than we might even realize. If we get stuck, however, believing that our modest bank account means we have only modest freedom, we are bound to miss out on our true potential for happiness. Getting a high-paying job or a big contract or even winning the lottery is not a path to freedom. You probably don't need more money in the bank to free yourself.

Reason #5: To Gain Love and Attention

Money can attract love and attention, but relationships gained through money are fragile and superficial at best. When the money runs out, the love, respect, and friendship go with it. And even though money can attract love, it so often has the opposite effect. People are often repulsed by others who flaunt their money or expect special treatment because they are wealthy. And that is because money is not all that people require or want to live happily. We require the things that are found at a deeper level.

When you try to gain love through your money, you base all your own worth on how much you have. And though it will impress some people, when it comes down to it, most people look for more in a friend or a lover than just wealth. So when your money fails to create deep and lasting relationships, your self-worth will suffer and all the money you've made won't be able to improve it.

People in this situation tend to start feeling paranoid about the friends they do have. They think that people want them around only because they have money. But money is what these people used to get respect and friendship in the first place.

Reason #6: To Express Love and Appreciation

Money is just a neutral energy—it can be a weapon when used with resentment and anger, or it can nurture with love and care. Money is a vehicle for our emotions and attitudes. People want money so they can express the love and appreciation they feel in their lives. This is an ideal reason to accumulate money, but there is actually something we should be careful about here.

Just because you don't have a lot of money, don't think you can't express love and gratitude for people. Big gifts are exciting, but we are really moved by the intention and feeling behind them. The amount of love given is not equal to the size or expense of a gift. We remember the emotional connections, our deep trust in people, the memories we have together.

And the energy of a positive relationship turns ordinary money into Happy Money. So when you do have the chance to use money in an act of love, you can be sure that it is money well invested. Happy Money compounds at a high rate of interest. The person you give it to uses it to generate more, and more eventually comes back to you. What matters is how the money inspires action.

HOW HAPPY ARE YOU WITH THE MONEY YOU CURRENTLY HAVE?

Are you happy with your financial situation now?

Do you feel blessed and energized about life when you think of money? Or do you feel frustrated when you think of money?

Do you think the reason you chose in the previous section has anything to do with your current relationship or feeling toward money?

I am going to share a little something with you: it doesn't matter how much you have or make. It is your feelings about money that determine your wealth. If you don't have a healthy attitude and you feel negative about money, then no amount of money in the bank is going to change your relationship with money.

WHAT'S IN YOUR WALLET?

If there is indeed Happy Money and Unhappy Money, what kind of money are you carrying around?

Check your wallet, just as the Mysterious Wallet Woman asked to do. Even though you can't see the smile of the money physically, you can pretty much guess if it is smiling or not.

If you are happy with your work and life, your money is more than likely smiling in your wallet.

If you hate your job and always complain about something in your life, your money is crying or angry in your wallet.

We all want our money to smile. If it isn't, then you have to ask yourself: *What is wrong with my life?*

You may not be satisfied with how much you make or how much you have. You may feel that your partner doesn't appreciate your hard work and complains too much about how little money you make.

IF MONEY WERE A PERSON, WHO WOULD IT BE?

If money were a person, there are several personas it could have. What would your money's personification be?

Would that person be gentle and kind, or mean and unfriendly?

Remember your experiences in the past. For some people, money can be a cruel force that deprives them of many opportunities. Money may have given others all they ever needed and wanted. Perhaps money gave you a few surprises in the past too. Maybe it came through your grandparents, a few scholarships, some foundations, or a generous bonus at the end of a tough work quarter. If money has always been kind to you, you feel safe knowing it will always be there in the future.

When people have had great experiences with money—as in, they could always count on it being there and trust that it will be there in the future—chances are they are having a great life. They may not be wealthy, but they seem to feel "blessed." Things just work out for them. When they imagine the future, it is not difficult to see a bright one.

For those who have not had good experiences with money, I am sorry that life's been unfair. I am sorry that things weren't easy in the past. But I can assure you that doesn't mean your future is fixed or that you can't turn your life around or change your feelings toward money.

Money can be bad, but it can also be good—very good. You may wonder why it is so different to different people. You may be wondering why some people have parents who help them pay for college and always seem to have their needs met, while others struggle to put food on the table.

I believe money changes its character according to the places and whose hands it is in. So when you are fearful, you project fear onto money—money is no friend to you. If you are happy, money is more likely a joyful force—it's always going to be there for you. If money has been tainted for generations with negative thoughts and beliefs, like those of scarcity, then you can be sure you'll never have enough money—unless, of course, you change the energy around the money you make, receive, and give away.

EACH OF US IS STUCK IN A UNIQUE MONEY DILEMMA

I have friends from all walks of life. I have friends who live as far away from money as possible and are enjoying their life in a forest. They grow their own food and spend only $1,000 a year. They do virtually everything without money, using it only for medical supplies and miscellaneous items they can't grow or make themselves. I have other friends who are extremely affluent and think nothing of spending $1,000 on wine or a casual lunch. I have friends who are elite experts in their fields—doctors, lawyers, and successful business owners who have several public companies. And I have friends who own mom-and-pop drugstores and small shops, work in factories, drive trucks, or do physical labor.

No matter whom I talk to from any walk of life, when I am interviewing them, invariably they start complaining about their life and ask me for advice. And, without exception, both the rich and the poor have similar worries and concerns, and almost all always feel overwhelmed by money.

But for different reasons.

The super-rich don't worry so much about money at the moment, but they worry about their future. They admit they are afraid their success may not last forever. They have seen many people who have failed on their way to the top and who have either lost all that they earned or were in a bad situation. They worry about their kids and complain about how they are not handling money prudently. Even all the money in the world doesn't prevent people from worrying about money.

Yet people with seemingly moderate amounts also have worries and complaints. People in the middle class tend to complain about money in a different way. Their biggest frustration is that the demand for their money and resources is often larger than their income. They feel stretched by the pressure of expenses. This is exacerbated if they have kids. They are in a constant battle with their children about allowances and how to spend money. On top of that, they have to save for their kids' education and worry that they won't have enough money of their own for a comfortable or happy retirement. On top of all this, they are pressed for time. They spend every waking moment either working for or worrying about money and how to balance it all.

Those in the lower middle class often feel like they are being taken advantage of: somebody is always trying to get something for nothing from them. They feel marginalized and undervalued in the working world. They don't think that the rich people who hire them realize the sacrifices they make to work hard for so little pay, while the rich enjoy the fruits of all their labor.

And, finally, the financially challenged or poor are just struggling to survive and can't even see past the need to get by. Money—never mind that having too much of it can cause other problems and worries—is a mystery to them. You often hear people say, "I'd like to have those rich-people problems." Yes, to a poor person who is hungry, the rich person's problems don't seem so terrible.

Regardless of our situation and our financial status in life, we all are affected by money one way or another. And how we react to our situation can make us happy or unhappy.

SO CAN MONEY BUY HAPPINESS?

People often hear the common expression "Money can't buy happiness."

If this is true, then why are so many people clamoring to make more money? Do they want to be unhappy? Why do so many people want money desperately? Why do some even go as far as to commit crimes in order to get more?

Needless to say, there are some great benefits to having money. When you ask five-year-old kids what they want, they usually answer something tangible, like candies or toys. But if you ask ten-year-old kids, they say, "Money! I will decide what I want to buy with it later!" So even young kids seem to figure out early that money is like some form of a magic wand that can create miracles.

It will turn into whatever you want it to be.

At the same time, we know money cannot buy happiness.

Maybe we want to believe this to comfort ourselves when we don't have money.

Yet, when we hear that some friends won money in the lottery or inherited money from distant relatives, we feel a pang of jealousy. We were fine moments before we heard the news, but as soon as we find out someone got something and we didn't, it suddenly doesn't feel so "okay" anymore. So we say "Money can't buy happiness," and we feel a little better about our plight without the Mega Millions jackpot payout.

TAKING A ZEN APPROACH TO HAPPINESS AND MONEY

The Zen approach to happiness invites us to think about ourselves not in terms of what we do or what we are worth or what we have, but in terms of who we *are*. And what are we? Human beings. Our purpose as humans is to "be." What does that mean? It means being present in the moment. It means being fully grateful and in alignment with where our bodies and minds are at one time. If you're present in the moment, you aren't thinking about the past—your mistakes, your issues, the harm done to you and getting angry about it. And if you're present, you're not thinking about the future—its unexpected outcomes, its potential for disasters. If you're not thinking about the future, you're not anxious, you're not fearful, and you're not stressed. So much of our stress, anxiety, and unhappiness about money comes from thinking about our past mistakes or harm done to us and needlessly worrying about all the uncertainty of the future. Our past and future selves rob our present selves of happiness when we allow ourselves to get derailed by these negative thoughts. Happiness, then, truly comes from within. So we can agree that money cannot buy happiness. Nothing can. However, I will contend that it is a lot easier to be present and free from anger about the past and worry about the future if money isn't such an overwhelming force in one's life.

I have interviewed so many people for my books. And not all of them are necessarily financially well-off. Yet, after interviewing them all, I did come to this conclusion: Money cannot buy happiness, but money certainly eases some of the discomfort in life. In other words, the less worry and stress you have, the more time you have to *be*.

If you have money, you don't have to worry all the time about whether you can pay the bills at the end of every month. You can treat your friends to something if you want. You can give a gift to your potential partner.

Though money certainly helps, it is not essential to happiness. There are several studies about how much one earns and its relationship to happiness, and they always show that people's happiness level goes up as their income goes up, but only up to about $75,000. Beyond this threshold, one's level of happiness doesn't go higher with any more income, because there will be more money-related stress compared to the joy that more money brings into one's life.

When I talk about this in New York and Tokyo, I get the same response. Everyone says, "There is no way you can make a happy living with that little money." And this can be true. The cost of living varies depending on where you live. But the important thing you should know is that making more money doesn't guarantee happiness.

This may make you wonder about people who make less than $75,000 in a year. The truth is, I have met people who are happy even though they can barely make ends meet. How do they do it? It's because they have a good relationship with money: it doesn't define who they are. They don't need it to keep up with the Joneses. And they don't stress out about the future or things they can't control. They don't believe in the myth of scarcity. They know they'll always have enough of what they need when they need it. They are okay with where they are and who they are. They aren't hypnotized into thinking that having a bigger house or a flashier car is going to somehow magically transform their life and take away all their problems. They know they have something to say about their own happiness. Money doesn't control or have power over them; *they* have power over *it*.

Most important, they aren't afraid of money.

Afraid of money? Who is afraid of money?

More people than you realize.

LOVE OR FEAR: YOUR RELATIONSHIP WITH MONEY

Some time ago, I translated Dr. Gerald Jampolsky's bestselling book *Love Is Letting Go of Fear*, in which he contends that there are two kinds of communication: love and fear.

And I contend that when it comes to money, there are two approaches to it: love and fear.

When you earn and spend money, you do it with either love or fear.

For example, we are afraid of money all the time. We are afraid that what we have may not be enough for a rainy day. We are afraid we may lose it. We're afraid others have more of it than we do. Or that if others earn more or get more, there will be less for us. We're afraid we might lose our jobs—if we did, how would we pay all the bills? Even when we spend money, we do so out of fear. *If I am not spending my money in a deliberate or smart way, I will lose money.* Sometimes we feel pressure when we spend money. We're afraid we're being taken advantage of, scammed— that we're spending too much, or what if we get the wrong thing and don't like it in a few months? We worry that if we buy one thing, we won't have enough for something else later.

Many of us let fear creep into our decisions without even realizing it. Granted, some of these fears are rational and there for a reason. The fears are tied to survival. If we mess up with money, we won't have a place to live, food to eat, or clothes to wear. Some people are born with a stronger sense of fear, or it is cultivated in their homes by their parents and relatives who have negative or fear-based relationships with money, while others don't have any fear at all. It doesn't seem to cross their minds that money will ever run out.

Since we were very small, we have been told to "do the right thing" with our money. Our parents didn't even know what that meant, but it didn't stop them from saying it. We were scolded about money—about what we spent it on, how we lost it, and how careless we were with it. We carry those fears with us into adulthood without even realizing it or recognizing how much fear is attached to our actions with money.

Unfortunately, our current financial system is based on fear. Our society is based on fear—our education system, our workplaces, and possibly our home lives too. We fear doing the wrong thing and being punished. We fear that others have what we don't have. So we become greedy. We fear resources are limited or scarce, so we take more than we should and waste more than we should. We fear that other children will get ahead of ours and have more advantages, so we send our kids to expensive schools and then complain about paying taxes for public schools. We are fearful enough that our kids will misbehave or embarrass us that we scold them and control them. Needless to say, using fear is not an effective way to get what you want. It is often destructive and causes lasting harm.

In a sense, it's no surprise that so many of us are fearful around money. It is an automatic response. If you don't pay much attention to your mind, you will hardly be aware that fear is what motivates your actions, whether at home, at work, in your community, or in the way you behave with money.

WHAT IT MEANS TO HAVE A LOVING, ABUNDANT RELATIONSHIP WITH MONEY

The opposite of fear is love. To love is to have no fear that something will harm or leave you. It requires your trust and belief that whoever is the object of your love will always be there. Most of us are told that our parents love us, but their methods of love might have been expressed more like fear. Their anxiety and worry held us back from trying new things. Their worry about money prevented them from letting us take chances in our careers or relationships. Fear looks, sounds, and feels like *control*. Love, on the other hand, feels like the opposite. It is *unconditional acceptance*. It's a willingness to trust that things will work out. It feels like letting go. Love feels a lot like just "being" in the moment— no anger about the past, no worries about the future. You're happy to be here now. You are grateful. Intensely grateful for all you have, and where there is gratitude, there is joy and enthusiasm. And joy and enthusiasm make you happy.

WHAT IT'S LIKE TO LIVE WITH A
LOVING RELATIONSHIP TO MONEY

It's hard for a lot of us to imagine what it looks like to have a worry-free, stress-free relationship with money. But let's imagine it for a second. I want you to imagine that it is possible to live peacefully with money.

People who live "in love" with money are *doing* what they love and make enough money. In fact, they often say, "I have enough" or "I have all that I need." They may not be rich, but they truly have everything they need. They put what they love in the center of their life. They are financially comfortable, so they don't feel stress around money in everyday life.

When they go to a restaurant or shop, they choose not by the price but by their preference. That doesn't mean they always buy expensive stuff. They are just choosy. They know what they want, so they don't need to buy many things. Nor do they need to buy expensive or brand-name things, because they're not looking to others for external validation. They are already happy with themselves, who they are, and what they want to be. Their relationships, then, are authentic. They hang around with people they like, not people they are trying to impress or who are trying to impress them. They have a good relationship with their family and can spend quality time with them, because they're not working so hard to make a few extra dollars. And though sometimes they feel money stress, they tell themselves, *This happens sometimes, and I am always able to get through it. It will all work out.* They know how to *let go* of stress and not control things out of fear of what could go wrong. They can separate what is real and what is not in regard to their fears when it comes to money.

Ultimately, these people choose how to approach money. They are deliberate in the response and reaction to it. *They are Zen.*

And we can all choose our approach to money, to our life. How?

I believe it begins with gratitude. Instead of believing there is never enough, you begin thinking: *I have all that I need, and I am so grateful for it all. I am grateful for the work I do, the food I eat, the car I drive, and all the money I make.* When money comes in, you say, "Thank you" or, as we say in Japan, "*Arigato.*" Even when money leaves you, you can say it again: grateful for how the money served you or what it is bringing to you now.

Whatever happens, you can say thank you. *Thank you* is a powerful phrase that will help you start to transform your relationship with money. The more you do this, the less stress you'll have and the more happiness will flow through you—and your money. And you'll begin to see, without much effort, how quickly the Unhappy Money in your wallet starts to grow and smile and turn into Happy Money.

CHAPTER 2

Money IQ and Money EQ

In my early twenties, before I had the good fortune of learning from my mentor Wahei, I started studying the concept of money intensively, reading any book that had "money" or "investment" in the title. I attended seminars and lectures of well-known businesspeople. In order to impress the speakers, I made an effort to pose interesting questions after the lecture and then followed up with a complimentary letter in which I asked them to take me on as their disciple or assistant. Most of the time these methods of flattery didn't work, but some of the recipients liked my passion and took me out for lunch and shared their knowledge and experiences with me. And it was from these encounters that I discovered that not all wealthy and seemingly successful individuals are the same. And that even though they look like they "have it all" from the outside, their real lives are quite different from the way they present them.

Once, while waiting for a new mentor of mine to show up for a scheduled meeting, I casually asked his secretary about him. She looked somewhat puzzled and said, "I just started working here, so I don't know him well." Not long after that, I learned that not many people stuck around long enough to get to know him. Because of his harsh and demanding attitude, people left his office only months after they started working for him. By the time I realized this, I was rushing to the door myself. However, other millionaires I met were warm, friendly, well respected, and loved by the people who worked for them, who had nothing but good things to say about their employers. These leaders are what we call "the real deal." A general rule I go by is that when the staff speaks ill of a leader behind his or her back, chances are he or she is not that decent of a person. You can get away with appearing wonderful to the masses for a little while, but the people you interact with on a day-to-day basis will always know who is "the real deal" and who is not. Having money and the trappings of success doesn't always equate to being a person who has something positive to offer the world. There's more to it.

But this brings up an interesting conundrum: Why are people who are phony, cunning, or shrewd seemingly so successful and wealthy? It doesn't add up. I wanted to get to the bottom of this. When I first started my investigation, I thought there was a clear path to becoming successful, a definite order to the steps you could follow. Simply put, the popular notion presented in a lot of financial books is this: You work hard and make money, save it, and invest it, and then someday you will be rich. I naïvely thought that would be the way I would do it too.

But is it that simple?

As you may already know, in reality, people who work hard and make a lot of money don't necessarily succeed in the traditional sense. Then there are those who are quite shrewd and cunning with money. The thing I realized about this second type of person is that their reputation eventually catches up with them. Trust me, word always gets around! And in the long run, being a con artist or even just a disingenuous businessperson doesn't pay. Sure, someone might succeed once or twice, but keeping up appearances simply isn't sustainable. And people in this category tend to be greedy: they want all the fame and attention and money for themselves. So they cut corners, pinch pennies, and withhold money from people who are deserving of it.

In contrast, I found that people with warm hearts and a sincere interest in benefiting others often succeeded in the long run. Generosity seemed to be their hallmark. In addition, they had a more relaxed attitude toward their money. One of my mentors said, "The key to success is, always lose just a bit every time you make a deal."

What he meant was that everyone walks away feeling good—and that the other party feels like he or she "won." As a result of this practice, he got a great reputation for being honest and sincere, always putting his business partners and clients first. No one ever felt like they were getting taken advantage of by him. Once he established this reputation, he never ran out of clients or business, because everybody wanted to work with him.

But was his story an aberration? I wondered. I had observed many cunning people, kind people, and everyone in between—great businessmen who never seemed to catch a break, successful business owners who seemed to make obscene amounts of money but lost it all, and successful people who didn't seem to have a clue as to what they were doing. I also witnessed people who never went to college and never even received basic knowledge on investing but found amazing success because they were great at what they did and clients liked them. Confused, I asked my mentor Wahei about my observations. He told me that financial wisdom consists of two parts: Money IQ and Money EQ. Money IQ (intelligence quotient) is focused on financial intelligence, which you obtain when learning about investing, tax law, and general monetary knowledge. Money EQ (emotion quotient) is the emotional intelligence required to deal with your reactions toward money.

Even though you may have an MBA education, if your Money EQ is low, you could very well end up losing money. That is why there is a long list of extremely intelligent individuals in this world with lots of letters after their names who have made bad choices and gone bankrupt. In order to achieve a Happy Money life, you need to have both a healthy Money IQ and a healthy Money EQ. Once you know about the intelligent and emotional aspects of making money, you will have a great relationship with it.

WOW!

I finally got it!

I felt the mystery of why some people have money and some people lose it was solved. But knowing this information and being able to do something about it are two different things. Since first learning this lesson from my own mentor, I've seen a thing or two in my day and even experienced times when I made and lost money, and I can finally say I've arrived at a place where I have Happy Money and live comfortably; some call me a Happy Little Millionaire. So how do you get your Money IQ and Money EQ up high enough so that you can live the life of a Happy Little Millionaire like me? I think the first thing you need to do is understand the basics.

MONEY IQ FROM THE PERSPECTIVE OF A HAPPY LITTLE MILLIONAIRE

Money IQ tends to be misunderstood as money management, but that is not its key function. Sure, it's necessary to understand the deeper meaning behind the intellectual aspect of money; that means looking at how you make, spend, protect, and increase it.

Making Money

Making money the way a Happy Little Millionaire would means doing the thing you love to do and sharing that gift or talent with others. When you put the most importance on being your sincere, true self and share your joy with those around you, you'll inevitably succeed. In order to make money, many people believe that they need to betray their own values or control others. Making money is not about finding ways to defeat the competition or more easily and effectively turn a profit. Making money means being true to yourself and then being able to share your abilities with the world. As a result, you spread joy everywhere you go, and the money you receive is simply an expression of your clients' or patrons' gratitude.

Spending Money

When you spend money like a Happy Little Millionaire with a high Money IQ, you don't do it with an eye to being thrifty. Instead your spending is always conscious. You're mindful of your true self and what makes you happy, and therefore you're able to put your money toward things that best express your desires. You don't want to waste your money on things that don't benefit your well-being. And because you've made these conscious choices, the result is that you never feel like your money is wasted. One of the best books that details and analyzes how people spend money that results in the highest levels of satisfaction is *Happy Money: The Science of Happier Spending* by Elizabeth Dunn and Michael Norton. They look at all the ways in which people spend their money, and those who spend on experiences that align with their values seem to be the happiest overall. They pored over studies and observed human behavior and found that those who were focused not on accumulating things but rather on experiencing things and being fully alive in the present moment (Zen!) felt the best about how they spent their money.

If spending money "well" means being thrifty or saving, then life can become a bit agonizing. In fact, life becomes a game of putting one's wants further and further away. You may want to investigate your instincts to be careful and thrifty: Why are you afraid to spend? Which of your fears are associated with spending? What price are you willing to pay for things that make you happy? When you assess your priorities and are mindful of activities that truly bring you joy, you can spend more confidently and know that the money you do spend is being used intelligently.

Protecting Money

Protecting money is less about hoarding it and keeping it away from others, and more about creating meaningful relationships around money and others—and keeping the boundaries between them clear. If you've ever felt that there are people in your life who have designs on your money—such as family, friends, employees, and clients—then the problem isn't with the money; *it's with your relationships*. If any one of these people would plot to take money from you, there is a problem. For example, one of the most common and costly causes of divorce is money issues. Either the husband or the wife tends to spend more than the other would like or can afford. Usually, one party keeps important financial information from the other in order to "protect" themselves or their money. The result: a fractured relationship, which inevitably leads to divorce. And in the attempt to protect their money, they end up losing more to begin with. (Anyone who has been through a divorce knows just how costly it can be.)

So the best way to protect one's money is to protect one's relationships with *people*. This obviously includes being clear and forthright on the terms of promises and always obeying the law. But the most important thing you can do is foster relationships in which you can communicate openly and honestly. If the relationships with the people around you are honest and clear, there is little need to protect your money far beyond that.

Increasing Money

When we talk about increasing money, most people automatically imagine investments and other techniques. However, for a Happy Little Millionaire, increasing money is more than just surface-level knowledge of the economy. Rather, it means finding a purpose that you believe in from the heart and then aiding that purpose with money. With a mind on the long term, you support your purpose in every way to make it successful. The important deciding factor in becoming a Happy Little Millionaire is to align your money with your values and convictions. Your investment practices should include your own activities and businesses. And the fruits of your labors—the profits—are yours to keep and enjoy. When you do this, you realize that markets will fluctuate, so you don't worry about investing during downturns or crises. You don't even consider whether or not you will profit, because your priority is to support people who share your values and vision. The long-term gain is always the same: you become successful because you're steadily investing, and eventually markets turn around. In the meantime, all the good Happy Money you invested and the causes and purposes you care so deeply about have flourished.

MONEY EQ FROM THE PERSPECTIVE OF A HAPPY LITTLE MILLIONAIRE

Money EQ is all about how we react to money emotionally. So it's necessary to understand the deeper meaning behind the emotional aspects of money. That means looking at how you receive, enjoy, feel confident about, and share your money.

Receiving Money

The act of receiving is the most important thing when it comes to enriching your life. If you aren't willing to receive happiness and abundance, then no matter how much money you have and no matter what high status you attain, you will never feel happy and abundant. Receiving means *allowing yourself the freedom to receive* and knowing that you have inherent value that is worthy of receiving good things.

I can't express how important it is to be willing to receive gifts, opportunities, and chances given to you. Oftentimes people fail to see the good things right in front of them instead of receiving them joyfully. They are so focused on a set outcome or their own negative beliefs, they miss amazing opportunities right under their noses and set themselves up for failure by chasing things that aren't meant for them. Have you ever been so preoccupied with working hard to earn the thing that you think you need that you missed out on something directly in front of you? If you shift your attention to the things that you can receive, you can begin to realize just how much you are given. When you open yourself up to receiving, that is the beginning of realizing true abundance.

Enjoying Money

When you appreciate something that you are enjoying, you become truly connected to the present moment: you are in a Zen moment. To be fully present and engaged is the definition of happiness. There is no past, no future, only the present—which is a gift. And when you are enjoying this gift, this present, you are experiencing this thing I have been referring to as abundance. However, most people do not feel this way. For most, life is a competition: even when they earn something, there isn't time to waste just enjoying it. They have to prepare for the next race! If they don't, they believe that maybe next time they will lose to someone else. People in this competitive/scarcity mind-set are disconnected from the present moment. They regret their past failures or worry endlessly and needlessly about the failures to come. The result is that they never get to appreciate and enjoy the fruits of their labor. Isn't that the same as having no fruits at all?

To experience abundance, you are required to be 100 percent in the present moment. In order to enjoy life and wealth, stop and smell the proverbial roses. If you're always rushing through each moment simply to get to the next, you're missing out on all the abundance that is available to you *now*.

Trusting the Money Flow

We worry about money because we are afraid and can't trust that money will always come in. To fully realize the potential of your life, it isn't just money and abundance that is important; confidence in your own abilities matters as well. Even when your supply of money is low, confidence and self-esteem lead to the heart of abundance.

Yet it wouldn't be a stretch to say that many people are overpowered by doubt. And the road of self-doubt leads to only one place: fear. Fear of trying new things. Fear of doing anything. Fear of sharing your skills and talents.

Fear of ridicule. If you want to become a Happy Little Millionaire, you have to muster confidence in yourself and your abilities.

People who are confident aren't that way because they're rich. *They are rich because they are confident!* You need to trust *before* you get money. All success is an outgrowth of confidence. And when we are able to trust the flow of money, both in and out of our lives, being confident comes naturally.

A big cause of money stress is that people don't trust the flow of money. They are worried that the money they make will not be enough to support their future. They worry that their ideas and projects won't be worth all the time and energy spent. But if we are going to be decisive and act with confidence, we have to accept that money is a fluctuating thing.

Sharing

When you are living like a Happy Little Millionaire, you know that life is something to be shared. Sharing your joy with people and offering your skills to them requires no hesitation. You know that sharing joy with people increases your own personal joy exponentially. Once happiness is experienced as something you do with others, you realize that there really is no other way to do it. Doing something solely for yourself is no longer interesting. Sharing should be part of every aspect of your life; whether you're sharing joy, money, services, or your gifts or talents matters little. It just matters that you do it—that you share! And that means sharing with everyone you meet: with your family, your friends, your coworkers, your clients, your customers, and society. The more you share and the more generous you are with your time, talents, and gifts, the more abundance will flow to you. Why? The principle of sharing is connected to natural law. The natural world is one of sharing. Everything is tied together mutually, and when one part suffers, the whole is thrown off balance. If many people were to become more open to sharing and partaking in the joy of life together, many of the world's problems would soon disappear. As Lynne Twist puts it so eloquently in *The Soul of Money: Transforming Your Relationship with Money and Life*:

> Money is like water. It can be a conduit for commitment, a currency of love.
>
> Money moving in the direction of our highest commitments nourishes our world and ourselves.
>
> What you appreciate appreciates.
>
> When you make a difference with what you have, it expands.
>
> Collaboration creates prosperity.
>
> True abundance flows from enough; never from more.
>
> Money carries our intention. If we use it with integrity, then it carries integrity forward.
>
> Know the flow—take responsibility for the way your money moves in the world.
>
> Let your soul inform your money and your money express your soul.

Access your assets—not only money but also your own character and capabilities, your relationships and other nonmoney resources.

MONEY EQ TYPES

Your relationship with money expresses itself in a pattern to a certain extent. If you've never been taught about money, you will likely fall into one of a few common personality types.

Knowing your own pattern is a means by which to understand the motivation behind the actions you take. The first step to creating a healthier relationship with money is to take an honest look at the map and acknowledge where you are standing right now.

When you understand the situation you're presently in, the next step is to turn around and research how you got there and where you came from. You may realize quite a lot about yourself in the process. Explore family secrets, stories from your mother's and father's youths, or even surprising facts about your grandparents when they were growing up. Researching your roots in this way allows you to understand yourself more deeply. Once you have identified your roots, you can reprogram yourself with new values that reflect who you truly are and who you would like to be.

From a Money EQ perspective, people who engage with money can be broadly separated into three types: the type who actively engages with money and tries to control it;

the type who tries to have nothing to do with money; and the type who actively tries to stay as far away from money as possible. I call the type who tries to have nothing to do with money the "indifferent" type, and the type who actively tries to stay as far away as possible the "monk" type.

There are also three variations of the type who actively engages with money, depending on how they try to control it: the "hoarder," the "spender," and the "moneymaking addict." These three subtypes, in addition to the first two types I named in the paragraph above, make up the five most basic money personalities.

Among the three personality types who actively engage with money, there are a few more common ones that show up as a combination of two or more of the basic types. For example:

Hoarder + Spender = the "Repressed Spender" type

This is usually someone who saves up a certain amount and then spends (blows) it all at once.

Spender + Moneymaking Addict = the "Gambler" type

Someone with this personality type earns a lot and doesn't hesitate to spend a lot.

Hoarder + Spender + Moneymaking Addict = the "Worrier" type

Someone who is a combination of all three active money types is most likely to spend every waking hour of their day worrying.

When it comes down to it, though, there are several distinct money personality types that are the result of varying combinations of all of the above. Let's find out which personality sounds vaguely familiar to you.

The Compulsive Saver (Stockpiler)

This Money EQ personality type absolutely loves saving money. Their favorite hobby is saving money. Their special talent also happens to be—surprise, surprise—saving money. If they saw a quarter on the street, they would pick it up and put it directly into their piggy bank at home. They believe saving money is the best way to guarantee a sense of security in life. It is so central to their way of life that their actual lifestyle is often quite frugal. They're usually experts on bargain shopping. They would be able to give you excellent advice on which phone company is the cheapest, which point cards are worth it, and when to buy plane tickets at the lowest possible price. This type of person feels most alive when they check their savings account and see that it is going up at a steady rate.

The Compulsive Saver type views enjoying the luxuries of life as a mortal enemy. In fact, it's usually a general rule that none of their hobbies or routine activities cost much money, if any at all. They have often forgotten the dreams of their childhood about how they wanted their life to turn out someday, no longer concerned with what inspired them to start saving in the first place.

The backstory to most Compulsive Savers comes from bad memories and fears about money from their childhood. They often grew up in a house without much money, suffering many painful or lonely experiences as a result. The family business may have gone bankrupt, or their parents could have been unable to earn enough money. It's very common for the effects of a bankruptcy in the grandparents' generation to carry down all the way to the current generation, passing along a fear that money will run out. If this personality type suffered due to their parents' poor relationship with money, they will often carry a strong determination not to turn out the same way. However, they are often unaware of or unable to recognize at what point fears about money took over and began controlling their lives. Compulsive Savers are convinced that their reasoning is sound and they are doing everything in just the right way.

If you think you might be a Compulsive Saver, it might be a good opportunity to finally confront your anxieties or fears about money and look deeper into when you developed them in the first place. No matter how much you save, it will never erase the unease you feel about money that motivates you to tightly hold on to as much as possible in the first place. Many Compulsive Savers are so afraid of running out of money that they will go their entire lives without spending any of the money they saved up for so long.

The Compulsive Spender (Spendthrift)

The Compulsive Spender type simply loves spending money. If this Money EQ personality type saw money on the sidewalk, depositing it into a piggy bank like a Compulsive Saver would never occur to them as an option. Compulsive Spenders would take it straight to the nearest vending machine and enjoy a free drink. They would also never understand Compulsive Savers' guilt over spending money on something, instead feeling uncomfortable setting money aside.

As friends, Compulsive Savers would be pretty boring to have around, but Compulsive Spenders will make sure you have the time of your life. They fully embrace "YOLO," the motto "You only live once." Many Compulsive Spenders have a friendly, outgoing personality and are fun to be around. They love giving gifts or treating people to something special for no particular reason. They will tell you that the reason for the economic downturn is that people have stopped spending money, and feel a strange sense of pride that they are single-handedly keeping the economy afloat. In extreme cases, Compulsive Spenders can be at risk of going bankrupt if they consistently spend more than they earn.

There is a reason that Compulsive Spenders behave the way they do. This personality type spends money in order to feel more in control. It's natural for people to feel a level of personal control over their surroundings whenever they purchase something. At the register, the staff responds politely with a bow (at least in Japan) and listens attentively to everything they have to say. It can give Compulsive Spenders a sense of self-respect or recognition of their worth as human beings that they may not often experience in other parts of their life. Compulsive Spenders often have low self-esteem and constantly feel as if they are suffocating. To escape from that feeling, they are quick to spend cash to release the pressure and brighten up their mood. However, this method keeps the suffocating feelings away only for a short time. The moment the clerk wraps up and hands them their purchase, that negative feeling begins creeping back in. Many Compulsive Spenders are unable to truly enjoy the things they buy. Several items of new clothing may end up permanently stored away in a closet without ever being worn a single time.

What's interesting about the Compulsive Spender type is that in most cases they were brought up by Compulsive Savers. The way they spend money comes as a judgment of or reaction to the suffocation or boredom they felt growing up with parents who enforced conservative spending.

The Compulsive Moneymaker

The Compulsive Moneymaker personality type believes life works best when they're earning as much money as possible. If this Money EQ type found some money on the sidewalk, they'd reassure everyone within range that it is proof that Lady Luck exists and that she is always on their side. This type of person spends the majority of their energy on improving their ability to make more money. They don't feel guilty about choosing to focus on work efficiency, time management skills, or business success over spending time with friends or family. This is partly because they truly believe that everything they're doing is for the sake of their families.

Compulsive Moneymakers live off approval and recognition from others for their financial success. Unfortunately, they'll never stop craving more of that attention, no matter how much money they make.

The Indifferent-to-Money Type

This type hardly realizes that money exists. If they come across a dollar in the street, they are likely to pass it without even noticing what it is. The Indifferent-to-Money person typically is found among professors, teachers, public servants, doctors, researchers, artists, and homemakers. They get on with life as though money is not an important factor. Daily life might look like waking up and taking their lunch box with them on the train to work, then spending the day focused on their tasks before returning home. Days can pass without their spending or giving much thought to money. The unconcerned/indifferent type will often leave managing finances up to a partner or spouse, to the point of being unsure of how much they really even have or where important financial documents are. They are simply unconcerned. Of course, this type does have to use money to live, but their hearts are not tied up in concerns over money.

Being quite well-off is a common characteristic of this type. For starters, they don't use money, so it naturally is saved. From when they were children, they were financially comfortable and did not give much thought to money one way or the other. It might also be said that this type is characteristically happy.

However, if the person who manages their system of finances is no longer there, tragedy can ensue. I once assisted an artist with legal affairs regarding his finances after his wife, who had always taken care of those sorts of things, suddenly passed. The man hardly knew where his wallet was and now found himself the only one responsible for his household's accounting. This unconcerned type is happy so long as they can afford to be unconcerned, but the reality of money responsibilities can—and often does—catch up with them.

The Hippie

This personality type basically thinks that money is a bad thing. If they found a dollar in the street, they would instinctively give it to charity or at least put it to use for a necessity. It would feel wrong for them to spend it on themselves.

Hippies tend to view money as a source of problems. They wish that the world could be less about making money and consumerism.

This type places a value on not "selling out" or selling

themselves for a price. They want to live lives that are as little affected by money as possible.

Saver-Splurger

This type is a combination of the saver and the spender. Saver-Splurgers are usually quite regimented and serious. But then suddenly they feel compelled to do something, to use their money. People around them are taken by surprise when this type of person, who is usually working and seemingly secure with their money, is broke again.

What this type is doing is trying to control their life through the saving of money. They go along and save diligently, believing it to be the best thing to do. But as though they can no longer hold their breath, it all comes out at once. The pendulum swings them from saver to spender.

When they do use their savings, they use it poorly, such as on things they don't need or won't use. They might consider buying a car even though they don't have a license. They might say, "It was going for a great price, so I figured I would just buy it now. I was thinking of getting my license soon anyway." I knew a woman who bought a professional aesthetician device for thousands of dollars. She said that she had put in a lot of overtime work and deserved something nice like this. But after buying it, she soon regretted it. She thought that, since she had it, she might as well use it; but for some reason just looking at it made her feel guilty, and now it remains in the closet.

The Gambler

This type looks like a combination of the Compulsive Moneymaker and the Compulsive Spender types. They like excitement and seek thrills. They are willing to take big risks, but are only happy with the wins and regret the losses. Gamblers' ends are not simply to increase their assets, although they may be convinced that they in fact are. The thrill of risk and promise of reward is a pleasure unto itself that this type can get lost in. And consequently this type is given to sudden windfall profits or devastating losses.

This is the type that gets excited by commodity trading and venture capital, and sees the monotony of consistency as a type of death. They might even say that they would rather die than live a life of monotony. I have observed that the Gambler is sometimes raised by the Compulsive Saver type. The boredom of living with parents who are so tight with money often sets a child on the path to becoming the Spendthrift or the Gambler.

The Worrier

This type is always worried about money. Regardless of how much money they have, they worry about it. They worry about the money they have being gone. When they don't have money, they worry about not having it.

Worriers do not trust life. They tend to expect that the future will be fraught with problems, and that causes them to worry. It is like worrying about the interest on a loan that you don't remember taking out.

This type also lacks confidence regarding the potential they possess as human beings. They lack self-esteem and the basic confidence required to execute tasks. Even when they are quite well-off, Worriers are concerned about some terrible thing happening and wiping them out.

It is important to mention that this type of worry is not directly linked to money. Rather, fear about life in general is being projected onto money specifically. As long as these fears go unresolved, concerns about money will not abate.

MOVING BEYOND YOUR PERSONALITY TYPE AND UNDERSTANDING THE FIVE NEGATIVE EMOTIONS KEEPING YOU FROM PROSPERITY

We have looked at reasons why many of us can't take a step into a Happy Little Millionaire's world, and we've examined the money personality types that are deeply connected to how we were raised. So how do we move past our limiting behaviors and beliefs around money? Is there a way to overcome our current status? I think there is, but it requires a bit more understanding of our current blocks that keep us from fully entering the present and being aligned with the abundance that is available to us. Here are some common blocks we all face:

1. Anxiety

Usually the most readily understood negative emotion is described as anxiety. Anxiety is the discomfort and uneasiness experienced when taking or planning to take an action.

There are two important things at work when it comes to anxiety. The first is a sense of discomfort when standing at the precipice of starting something new. Even though the feeling manifests as a negative emotion, it is also an indication that change is near.

The second thing is that this discomfort can and often does bring up other negative emotions that were more deeply hidden. Anxiety is one of the easiest emotions to be aware of. As we search for the reasons we are anxious, we discover feelings we might have been ignoring. Anxiety is often a sign that we need to pay more attention to our emotional state.

2. Fear

So many of us fear change. We fear losing friendships and love, and we fear loss itself. For this reason we put considerable effort into managing our risk of loss.

Optimistic people fear the idea of feeling fear. If they are seized by fear, they get the overwhelming sense that everything is going to fall apart, and they are naturally averse to thinking about anything that brings about such emotions. But running from fear is not the way to defeat it; only by meeting it head-on can we begin to have control over fear.

3. Doubt

When we set out to do something new, an accompanying feeling that we might not be able to handle what is to come is not uncommon. This is doubt. The voice of doubt can also come to us from others. A friend or family member might imply a comparison with ourselves and someone else, causing us to feel uncertain about who we are. With a little extra introspection, we can see that regardless of what seems to be the cause of doubt, it comes from within ourselves.

Doubt is what holds us back from entering a new world. When someone is against us or criticizes us, it is a chance to discover the doubts that we hold within ourselves and come face-to-face with them.

4. Guilt

There is a certain type of person who needs everyone around them to agree with them. This is because they feel guilty about leaving anyone out. When we feel guilt, it feels like we have done something wrong. But if we get the approval and agreement of others, then the negative feelings of guilt can be avoided. Yet the disapproval of one person can outweigh the approval of ten others. It is a feeling that can paralyze one's personal progress.

5. (Self-)Neglect

The last emotion on the spectrum of negative feelings is lack of self-worth or self-esteem. Without self-esteem, a happy and wealthy life is not possible. Even if happiness and wealth were to fall in one's lap, a lack of self-worth will prevent one from ever truly receiving or experiencing it.

Resolving our negative feelings about ourselves—and money—is the key to opening ourselves to all sorts of possibilities. When we operate in a state of anxiety, fear, doubt, guilt, or self-neglect, we are literally blocking the flow of energy and good fortune in our lives. If our eyes are focused on all that can go wrong, we can't possibly see the opportunities waiting for us. When we succumb to self-doubt and are down on ourselves, it's impossible to put ourselves out there and achieve great heights.

The sooner you realize that the only thing limiting you is . . . well, *you*, by your negative thinking, the more quickly you can move into a place where you can increase your Money IQ and Money EQ and your overall sense of peace, prosperity, and abundance.

HOW TO INCREASE YOUR MONEY IQ AND MONEY EQ

Many people think Money IQ is important. But after counseling individuals and witnessing how they have changed over the past twenty years, I think Money EQ is far more important than Money IQ.

Many money mistakes are related to emotions. You can be the smartest person in the world, but if you don't have a handle on your emotions and how they affect your behavior, it's impossible to make clear, good decisions related to money. One way to do this, I believe, is to become aware of your emotions, your innate proclivities and personality type, and then to seek out a mentor who can help you assess your relationship with money and guide you throughout your career.

You may feel there is nobody near you to match that description. I felt the same way thirty years ago. However, when you ask around, you will be surprised by how quickly such a person shows up. It could be your best friend's uncle or your colleague's cousin. This stage could be the hardest one. You may feel shy about it, or you may not want your friends to know about your sudden interest in money. But you have nothing to be embarrassed about.

In fact, I want you to be proud that you are setting out on a journey. It will be a road that your friends and loved ones can walk after you. I have felt a sense of pride my whole life. I was the first one in my family to go to college, and I was proud of myself for that. When I retired to raise my daughter, everybody was shocked and puzzled. In Japan, when your wife is pregnant, it is time to start working hard. It is not the time to leave work! But after I wrote about my experiences, many young Japanese fathers retired for their newborn babies as well and began a movement of sorts for men to become more involved in the raising of their children, and I was proud of that fact. I became a mentor to them, and many turned around and became mentors to those around them. It's important to reach out and find someone who can guide you. And I truly believe in the old saying "When the students are ready, the teacher will show up."

If you are ready, he or she will show up.

PATHS TO FINANCIAL FREEDOM

There are a few ways to be financially free. One is to get out of modern society. I have friends who do that. They live in the country and grow their own food and spend very little money. You don't have to worry about money if you choose that lifestyle. You don't need to dine out at a Michelin-starred restaurant or wear fashionable clothes. Instead you can eat organic carrots and other veggies and wear a comfortable fleece. You can commune with birds.

Some people dream about that kind of happy lifestyle. And there are many others, especially city people, who cannot imagine doing such a thing. To each his own, as they say.

The other way is creating cash flow that enables you to have enough assets and income to live your dream life. That is another way of living financially free.

If you want to take this route, you need to optimize your Money IQ and Money EQ, and when you do this you are going to work more creatively, you're going to spend money only on things you truly find important (because you've identified what matters), and you're going to be able to keep your mind in the present and be incredibly grateful for every moment of your life. You're also going to want to use some of the following tips:

Don't Save Money out of Anxiety

Many people save money because they are afraid of the future. They may get sick or lose their jobs, so they save for a rainy day. That is why people want to save: in case something bad happens.

But if you save money out of anxiety or fear, you will just feed more fear and anxiety—more blocks to the flow of money.

The side effect is that no matter how much you save, anxiety around money will not disappear. If you are broke, you may think you need to save enough money for a week so you can feel at ease about money. But if you have a week's worth of savings, you will feel like you need money for a month. After that, you may need a year's worth, or two years' and then five years' worth. It never ends. Even if you could save enough for the rest of your life, you would start worrying about the possibility of losing it all.

So your anxiety never disappears. Why? It is not related

to money at all. *It is anxiety and fear deeply rooted in your psychology.*

We think our fears are about money, but in reality it is the future and change we're afraid of.

Is there a solution to this madness? If you are going to save money, save it while you imagine the many fun ways to spend it. You might go traveling, eat at a nice restaurant, get a massage, retire in a desired location, spend it on your children and loved ones. See the difference? You're infusing your thoughts of money with appreciation, love, hope, and positive energy, thus ensuring that more will flow. You realize your money is there to support your joy and fun. If you start imagining all the fun things you can do with the money you are saving, you won't be able to worry at the same time. The human mind is very simple: it cannot process two emotions at once. Keep your mind focused on the fun, positive, and hopeful things. Your savings account—and your mind—will thank you.

You Will Lose Money Before Attracting Money

This may sound strange, but it is true. I have interviewed thousands of millionaires all over the world, so I have a lot of data that confirms this. In fact, I did a study with Kodansha, one of the prestigious publishing houses in Japan, called *How Ordinary People Became Millionaires*, which examined 10,000 millionaires and how they achieved success. I discovered many things, one of which was that they all lost much and experienced failure and loss before accumulating wealth. They lost in various ways: through bad investments, through theft by employees, or through failed businesses.

So don't get discouraged by the first misfortune. Think of it instead as getting one step closer to success. For after losing some, you will start attracting money—if, of course, you maintain a positive attitude and are open to receiving future success.

Likable People Attract Money

Other findings are that people who love what they do are far more likely to be successful than those who are unfulfilled in their work.

People who do what they love have more passion, go the extra mile for their clients, and serve more. They are more appreciated and respected by their clients and customers.

In a word, they are *likable*.

If you want to have a higher Money EQ, you need to love people. The more you care for others, the more you will receive.

People respond to someone who cares. Money will flow to these people. If more people like you, more money will flow.

Pricing Your Services Accordingly

I often get questions from freelance people about pricing. They often wonder what the right price for them is. They are not asking the question of *how*. They want to know more about how to price higher and still get clients and customers. They are afraid to raise their prices because they fear they'll lose potential clients.

It is scary to "put a price on yourself." The same goes when you ask for a raise.

What is interesting is that whatever price you set, you will get clients. However, they won't be the same: different people have different needs and abilities. If you price low, you'll attract those who can pay those prices; if you price high, you'll lose lower-paying customers but you'll attract those who are willing to pay higher prices.

So the question is: Are you ready for higher prices and attracting different clients and customers?

Arigato *and Learning to* Maro *Up*

People often assume that bigger is better. However, people who desperately aim for big money and riches often fail, and with that failure comes a lot of stress. When it comes to body weight, a lot of people say they want to lose some pounds. You won't hear so many people saying they want to gain weight, but occasionally you will find someone who feels great in their own skin, just as they are.

In terms of money, I have heard many people say they want more but rarely has anyone ever said they have too much. I've met only one man who said he had *enough*. I have mentioned my mentor Wahei Takeda a couple of times. I wrote about having "enough" in a book called *Maro Up!: The Secret of Success Begins with Arigato* with Janet Bray Attwood. Before Wahei's death, I had the privilege and honor to learn from him, and he was by far the happiest person I have ever met. Although most people around the world are unfamiliar with this great man, to put it in relative terms, he was like the Warren Buffett of Japan. He used to run one of the largest candy companies in the country, and what made his candy company so unique was that the factory workers listened to children singing *arigato*, which means "thank you," as they made this special and popular candy for babies. Wahei felt that the energy that came from the children singing while the factory workers were making the candy was why his candy was a bestseller. And I believe my success is a direct result of Wahei's philosophy of saying *arigato* consistently and applying his "*maro* up" philosophy to my own life and business.

So what is *maro*? The word is short for *magokoro*, which means "true or sincere heart" in Japanese. You could say *maro* is strong in those who have a pure heart and lead an upright life. Even in Japanese, it's hard to define *maro* because it's a spiritual state, but it could be called a state of selflessness, the opposite of ego. It can be thought of as the deeper end of one's consciousness, closer to the collective consciousness, the level at which all of humanity and the universe are one. As such, *maro* is the wellspring of our unconditional love for others, and also for ourselves.

Achieving a state of *maro* is the key to success. Wahei said that those who are in touch with *maro* always create win-win situations for themselves and the people around them. It follows that if you have a pure heart and true sincerity, not only will people treat you better but you'll begin to feel the whole universe support you as well.

When your *maro* increases, Wahei says you "*maro* up" and invite many miracles into your life.

WHAT *MARO* LOOKS LIKE

When your *maro* increases, you:

- become more magnetic, both emitting and attracting positive energy. This surrounds you with good people and things you care for deeply, which then creates a cycle of happiness and abundance.
- become more passionate and more energized to do the things you care about the most. You become more intuitive, and you can choose the best way to live your life. And since you are doing what you love most, you are constantly opening doors to exciting new opportunities and more abundance.
- express more gratitude for life. So you find yourself saying "thank you" more than ever before. Your gratitude is contagious, and you make those around you full of positive energy. As a result, others start to express gratitude and welcome more abundance into their own lives as well.

MORE ON WAHEI AND WHAT
WE CAN LEARN FROM HIM

Wahei Takeda was born in Nagoya, Japan, in 1932. The son of a local confectioner, he was taught by his father how to make cookies and sweets from a young age, and before long he was managing the family business. Wahei's creativity drove the business, and when he offered the first cream-filled sandwich wafer in Japan, it was a huge hit. After his success in the confectionery business, he expanded into real estate and investing, eventually becoming so wealthy as to be known as the Warren Buffett of Japan.

Wahei decided to devote more time to fostering the growth of small businesses, becoming what he called a "community philanthropist." Throughout his phenomenally successful career, his philosophy of *maro* inspired thousands of others to become more generous and open to the flow of money both into and out of their lives.

Wahei believed that kindness, generosity, and gratitude were the keys to happiness and prosperity. Inspired by the wisdom of the Shinto religion, he closely examined how people could invite good fortune into their lives. As he thought about the differences between happy and unhappy wealthy people, he recognized that the reason he felt happy was that he was always content with what he had. He wasn't consumed by greed; rather, he saw how he could bring abundance into other people's lives too. Inner contentment and gratitude are the essence of his philosophy of *maro*.

Personally, I feel that I have enough money to be happy and abundant. I also believe money will always come to me in perfect time. We don't have to wait until we have all the cash in the world to start living our lives. We just need to know when to turn left and when to make a right turn, getting just what we need exactly when we need it. A lot of people wish they had mountains of reserves of money on hand so they'd never have to worry for the rest of their lives, but too much money can actually be more of a burden than a blessing if your container is not the right size.

When I was doing accounting work, I saw many wealthy families who suffered from the burden of having too much money. The children of rich parents often ran into difficulties in life. Their parents had large amounts of money because they worked hard, achieved their goals, and made good connections with other people. However, sometimes their children suffered because they desired too much; their needs were so big, they were unable to find their own purpose in life. It was easy for them to get involved with drugs or alcohol, never finding what would truly bring them joy.

All the millionaires I've ever met who were also truly happy found their happiness not through money but through doing what they loved. They worked because they loved it.

The children of happy and prosperous parents tend to do well later in life because their parents choose to spend more time with them rather than overworking at a job they don't truly love.

The children of unhappy wealthy parents often inherit money without discovering what brings them happiness on a personal and professional level. This happens in part because the parents often devote too much of their time in their business trying to earn more money. If they feel lost in life, working only for the money, their business may grow, but they will probably not have spent as much time with their children as they would have liked.

YOUR MONEY BELIEF SYSTEM

Although Wahei taught me his philosophy about money, my father taught me useful and meaningful approaches as well. He taught me that there is a reason why successful people are successful and a reason why unsuccessful people don't achieve success. Successful people continue to succeed, building on their success, while unsuccessful people keep stumbling over weird misfortune and "bad luck."

There is a Japanese saying that you can be "born on Planet Poverty." Many people believe that being poor is just fate, but my father explained to me that there is a bigger factor at play: *It's how you think about work and money—not fate—that determines your wealth*. If your attitude toward your job and finances is off, your life will follow suit.

If your money blueprint is full of happiness and joy, helping others and reaping rewards, then you will be wealthy. If it's full of anger, hatred, bad memories, and feelings of competitiveness, your life will be filled with those same ingredients.

At the same time, people are conditioned to get money in certain ways. If you work for a company and get fired, more likely than not you will search for another job and begin working at a different company. A business owner whose business fails won't apply for a job and start working for someone else; they will start another business and try again. However, it may not cross their mind to invest in the stock market. Investors never consider working for someone else or running a company; they just look for another place to invest their money. And, sadly, people who never work or know what to do with money continue not to work or know what to do with money. People function exactly according to their "money blueprint," which is to say, what they have learned or come to know.

My father told me that every person *should learn* how they feel about money. Prosperous people experience feelings of happiness when they think about or physically touch money. *They actually feel joy.* On the other hand, people without money feel uneasiness or dread when they think or talk about it, and that's where the feelings of confusion originate.

At the age of twenty, I decided to achieve financial independence before the age of thirty, so I began my quest for the keys to happiness and success.

I had heard an old adage that went something like "All the money you make in your twenties will be lost by the age of thirty." As an optimist I found that hard to believe, but it turns out that all those wealthy people were right.

I had gained and lost my fortune (I thought at the time) repeatedly in my early twenties.

Instead of just desperately trying to make more money, I knew I had to fix the source of the problem if I wanted to break out of the pattern. It was futile to play the game according to the same rules that were making everyone else miserable. I realized that the most important puzzle piece would be to discover what was written on my own money blueprint and to rewrite the parts that were working against me.

Most of us are probably well overdue for a review of what is written on our money blueprints. We've already established that what we learned when we were younger has had a powerful effect on us. *But that doesn't mean we can't change it.* Every once in a while it's time for a revision or an upgrade to a newer version. If you were influenced by your parents, as we all tend to be, your money blueprint was drafted from the time you were young. Your parents' money blueprint may have been heavily influenced by your grandparents. If they were small in the 1930s, then no doubt it is full of fear and apprehension that stemmed from years of difficulty following the Great Depression that were then passed down through the generations and continue to influence you quietly to this day.

Your grandparents taught your parents that spending money foolishly could later equal death. If you didn't want to lose your job, you had to hang on to your money without spending a dime. Treating money as a source of security was the mentality of the 1930s, when few people had jobs and everyone was scared. That scary feeling your grandparents had when they were small never disappeared, even when they had children of their own—and so they passed that fear on to them, who in turn raised us.

The problem with money blueprints is that the code was written decades ago and has a tendency to stay hidden deep inside, popping up only when you feel scared or afraid. It comes up when you make an important decision in life. When you marry someone or change jobs, this feeling surfaces without you noticing.

But the thing about blueprints is that they are just a design—a shell, if you will. You can erase the lines and start over. The structures aren't built yet. The steel beams aren't welded together; the foundation hasn't been poured. You have plenty of time to amend the design and create a blueprint from which you can build a solid financial future.

FINDING THE RIGHT CONTAINER SIZE

Once you've established how you feel about money—what you believe about money—and have healed your past relationship with money, it's time to start looking at where you see yourself and money in the future.

Inside each of us there are, in the metaphorical sense, many containers. There are containers for abundance, money, happiness, relationships, work, and many other things. These containers are like open jars. If they are only half-full, we tend to feel unsatisfied. If the amount flowing in is more than our container can handle, it will overflow, and we accept only as much as we think we deserve. The goal is to feel as Wahei did: *That you have enough. That you are grateful for everything you do have, and you feel you can give some away.*

What this all boils down to is the importance of finding the right container size for you. Some people have very small containers but hold on to money tightly, while others have broken and cracked containers that leak.

There are ways to gauge the size of the money container within each of us. For example, maybe you make $100,000 a year but feel unsatisfied, yet the energy you spend trying to earn $150,000 burns you out; your container size is somewhere between $100,000 and $150,000. If you make $50,000 but feel bored with your life, that means you have a bigger container but you're not filling it all the way up. If by some fortunate circumstance you were born with the gift of money, you should go for it and aim higher and higher. If not, it's wise to know the limit where you find the most happiness.

That is what it means to have a money container. If you try to fill it past its capacity, at best you may break the container and make yourself miserable in the process. Most of us are brainwashed into always wanting more, and that's how we lose our peace of mind.

THERE'S NO PEACE TO BE FOUND
IN ALWAYS WANTING MORE

A healthy relationship with money can bring you a deep sense of peace. We live with the delusion that becoming rich will make us happy, solve all our problems, and put our worries to rest. The truth is actually completely the opposite. The more money we earn, the larger our work or business grows. When companies get bigger, expenses and payrolls get bigger too. It gets harder to keep things running with the same amount of effort as before, and so our troubles and stress increase along with that growth.

For example, many people in Japan believe that they would be able to live a prosperous and easy life if they had a monthly income of about $1 million. And why not? That sounds like more than enough. But when our income grows that large, we tend to want to buy bigger homes or cars or increase other lifestyle expenses because we think we can afford it.

The people you spend time with also shift as you become friends with more people at your earning level, so you find yourself going to more expensive restaurants rather than risk insulting someone by going to the cheap restaurant you used to love when you were a starving college student. Ultimately, what ends up happening is that your expenses increase just as much as your income does, so when a month comes along with less-than-stellar profits, you feel the stress of not having enough money. Can you imagine that?

Things would look very much the same even if you earned $3 million a month. At each level of wealth, there will always be someone earning more than you and doing things on a larger scale. If you continue climbing up that ladder, eventually the friends you meet will start saying things like "I was going to take my family out to Hawaii this weekend on our private jet. We're thinking of building a summer mansion there."

Your circle of friends will naturally keep raising your lifestyle level higher and higher, as it's in our nature to develop habits and grow more similar to the people close to us.

Someone living in a big city might know what it's like to walk to the train station and suffer the morning commute, eventually trading up to catching a taxi to work when they can afford it or eating at nicer restaurants for dinner simply because they feel money is not a problem like it used to be. Before you realize it, even though your salary may be several times larger than it was when you first started working, the amount you have left over at the end of the month remains constant, because your spending has gone up too!

So a salary of $1 million a month in no way guarantees financial freedom. Our toys just get more and more expensive.

It's worth a word of warning here that business comes and goes in waves. It's easy to forget about that when things are going well, but no matter how successful you are, there will always be times when income goes down a little. Many successful people tend to think optimistically and have difficulty adjusting when the winds change.

The reality is that no matter how much your income or assets increase, there really isn't going to be a time where you can just relax and let it all go. Even with a certain amount of savings in the bank, there will always be issues or problems that need your attention, such as changing the direction of your business, lawsuits, trouble with employees, taxes . . . the list goes on.

When you get into the cycle of wanting more, it takes away your ability to recognize what is truly most important in your life. When business or work is going particularly well, a lot of people even get addicted to the excitement. It almost turns into a game, and as in a game we start feeling the illusion that our worth as a human being goes up with each new level or achievement. We can easily spend more time at work at the expense of enjoying time with our families or personal interests.

Do you understand what I mean when I say there is no "winning" or satisfaction to be found in the game of continually wanting more?

HOW CAN YOU CHANGE YOUR MONEY LIFE?

I have read hundreds of books on money. In fact, at my retreat center in Japan there are thousands of books I have collected all my life on money, wealth, and happiness. The money books are primarily divided into two categories: technical books and mental attitude books. The technical books focus more on Money IQ and financial ins and outs. By the tenth page, you may feel beaten up many times and feel like giving up. The other kinds of books are focused on mental attitude: they focus largely on the law of attraction—for example, if you imagine a million dollars and believe it will be yours, it will be attracted to you. Although I am a believer in the law of attraction and the importance of a positive mental attitude, I also know that it doesn't happen that easily. Nevertheless, it can't hurt to have a positive attitude.

YOU CAN CHANGE YOUR BELIEFS AND THE SIZE OF YOUR MONEY CONTAINER

As you now know, you can create your own money blue-print, because you can change your mind-set, beliefs, and behaviors. You can do this by reckoning with your past, healing your past money wounds through forgiveness and appreciation—which I will walk you through in the next chapter. Eventually you make a decision about the kind of relationship you want to have with money and then ultimately about what feels most comfortable to you. You can create a new life.

I have taught these lessons to tens of thousands of people, and I personally witnessed their financial transformation. It can get better, and you can make that happen.

If you could choose your future, what would you want it to be?

I don't want you to push yourself too hard. If you are in debt, imagining a debt-free life is good enough. If you can imagine a better future, that is great too. I want you to believe that could be your future. I have seen it happen. For example, one of my clients inherited his father's business, which was in very bad shape. He could have said no to inheriting both assets and debts, which many people would have done. But he didn't want his father's legacy to be that of a failure. Still, after a few years of working so hard and not going anywhere, he was losing hope. So he came to my seminar. He realized that he was holding on to a false belief that no matter how hard he worked, he would never have enough money. As a result of attending my seminar, he realized that this wasn't just his belief: *it was his father's as well.* It was no surprise that his father's business and finances were in such disarray. He believed that they always would be no matter what he did. Upon recognizing that this negative viewpoint hadn't worked for his dad, he suddenly realized it wouldn't work for him either. He didn't have to make the same mistakes his father had made. He changed his perspective, his blueprint, and his container. Ultimately, he decided to become a money magnet. I gave him some advice. I asked him to imagine in his mind the amount of his current debt. It was $3 million. I told him to feel the impact of that number, and then to put a minus sign in: "−$3,000,000." He laughed and did it in his imagination. I told him, "Did you realize that you became a millionaire in two seconds! Your father didn't leave a debt. He left a company to you. So you have the power to make money." He made the decision right then and there that he would pay the debt in five years. After that session, his financial situation got infinitely better. He paid off all the debts! And he didn't stop there. He kept earning more, and within a few years he became a millionaire! If this man could turn his fortune around in a few years, I know you can change your life too. You cannot do it in a day, but if you shift your focus and keep going in the right direction, you will create your ideal life.

PRINCIPLES TO REMEMBER WHILE TRYING TO ACHIEVE A HIGH MONEY EQ

Knowing That Doubt Is Part of the Game

We often believe that success will erase our fears and doubts. Yet just when we rid ourselves of the fears and doubts in one area, the next brings a new set of anxieties. It would be great if we could go about our business feeling happy and optimistic each day. However, the reality is that most days bring with them a lot of things to worry about.

So rather than be consumed by the doubts that come to us, we can be prepared to handle them if we recognize that they are natural occurrences. Otherwise, we might believe that the presence of these worries and doubts in our minds means that we are doing something wrong.

In order to be ready to coolly and calmly deal with these feelings when they arise, we must understand that doubt is a part of business. Fears and doubts are not necessarily bad things. They are actually signs that we are in the process of developing new potential.

Seeing the Positive Side of Worry

The next principle is to practice feeling anxiety in a positive way. We instinctively pull away from negative emotions. But as we just discussed, anxieties are something that will always arise. To escape them, you would have to completely shut out your emotions, which would leave you feeling nothing. You would also throw away your ability to feel joy and wonder.

Joy and anxiety are emotions that come as a set. Running from fear robs you of life's wonder.

Believing in a Vision

The third principle is to always believe that there is a better future. As you go ahead in life and business, fears and doubts will come into your mind, and it is at those moments that believing in the future becomes key.

Help from a mentor or friend is important at times when you cannot bring yourself to truly believe that a better future is possible. It is relatively easy to trust in the future when the idea is reinforced by your support network.

Life holds the opportunity for us to have all kinds of marvelous experiences. Truly trusting in life and its possibilities lays the groundwork for making it a reality. Our state of awareness is a powerful influencer of reality. And when you trust in a better future, you are able to give hope to others who are dealing with their own fears. Truly trusting in a vision for the future is a way to help many other people. When we are calm and collected, sharing our abilities with others is rather simple. But the real test is to be able to share ourselves despite our doubts about ourselves and our worries over our own wealth and future.

Overcoming Your Emotions About Money and Sharing the Experiences with Others

The fourth principle is always to be sharing. The times when we are really feeling negative emotions are the times when our state of awareness is put to the test.

Continually being present for others and ready to share with them in the face of personal doubt is what powers us through those negative emotions. But this is no easy task. When it seems really tough to put this idea into practice, try to make a plan for how you can be present for others. Thinking about a plan and keeping it with us daily eventually influences our actions and outcomes.

Being present for other people is a testament to the level of trust that you have in your abilities and your future.

Being Open to Receiving Support and Love from Others

The last principle is to receive the love and support of others with your sincere heart. When you are experiencing negative emotions, getting through it on your own can be nearly impossible. But with the love and support of others, problems that seemed big at the outset start to shrink to a manageable size and become easier to sort out and handle. We already discussed seeking help from friends and mentors in order to believe in a better future.

We tend to believe that unless we do something for others, we cannot get support from them. In fact, it is a beginning. Being open to receiving help is a powerful step in the right direction. If you allow yourself to receive support unconditionally, you will begin to understand that you can share and help others as well. The love and support of our friends has the power to lessen anxieties that would otherwise consume and paralyze us.

CHAPTER 3

Money and Your Life

DO YOU USE MONEY OR DOES MONEY USE YOU?

At our kitchen table many years ago, my father said to me, "Money has two faces, like a coin. God and the devil."

I had many conversations with my father when I was little. Over the dinner table he'd talk to me about business, money, politics, and what was going on in the world. However, the way my father spoke that day was sort of unsettling. I remember that I felt as if I had overheard something I wasn't really allowed to know.

Even as an adult I can see what my father was referring to whenever I look at a newspaper or television and get the feeling that there could be something darkly magical about money. It seems like every criminal case both real and fictional revolves around money in one way or another.

More than once you've probably heard stories about ordinary hardworking employees who found themselves over their heads in debt due to a gambling addiction. Somehow the situation always seems to escalate to abuse of company funds, bribery, fraud, and sometimes even violence and murder. How could this happen just because of money? It makes you feel as if money has a strange and dangerous power to take an average person and suck them into a world of insanity.

The friends and family of that person will tell you, "He was such a calm person, until money became involved and rationality went out the window." Perhaps, rationality "goes out the window" because money is so intimately connected to our lives and how we define ourselves and our values as people.

Anyone can be affected by similar money stress, the kind that seemingly causes a sort of temporary insanity. Who hasn't lost sight of who they truly are and done things they would consider crazy under normal circumstances—all because of money? Not everyone will necessarily resort to stealing or hurting someone, but it's not uncommon to do crazy things for money—like unhappily continuing to work at a job doing something just for the sake of paying your bills, or sucking up to customers or coworkers with insincere words to ensure a steady flow of income.

If you don't gain an awareness about the extent to which money is influencing and controlling your current lifestyle and decisions, it's impossible to break free from money's grip over you.

In order to release this grip, I believe you need to understand and know exactly how you approach money. And there are only two approaches you can take: you can either use your money well or allow your money to use you.

WHY WE ARE SO CONTROLLED BY MONEY: FACING OUR PASTS

When my daughter was in kindergarten, I used to volunteer in her classroom a few times a week. I enjoyed watching over the children and watching them grow. And while I was there, I was able to sit back and make some observations.

When we are born, we don't automatically come equipped with an opinion one way or the other about money. Our interest emerges much later, around the time we start going to kindergarten and playing with a variety of other children. This is generally the case regardless of what country you grow up in. Of course, there are many small differences between the Japanese and Western educational systems, but there are far more similarities, including the beloved Christmas holiday vacation.

Japan shares the West's enthusiasm for decorating and preparing for the Christmas holiday well in advance. Stores begin switching out orange and yellow candies for red and green ones as early as the first of November.

The year my daughter was in kindergarten, the classroom was lit up with lights and decorations as the holiday drew near. The cold weather outside made the indoors seem warmer, and in that cozy environment it was easy to let the Christmas spirit in as well. While the children were playing games one afternoon, I asked one of the boys what presents he was going to get for Christmas.

Matter-of-factly, the child responded, "I'm not going to get any."

That wasn't exactly the type of answer I was expecting. Was he on Santa's naughty list this year? Maybe this boy wasn't fooled by tales of Rudolph and workshop elves. Curious, I asked, "Why not?"

"Because my family is poor."

Poor?

Calculating the likelihood of this six-year-old boy having a firm grasp on social and economic problems at his age, I asked him if he knew what the word "poor" meant.

He didn't.

"Where did you learn that word?"

He had heard his mother say it. She told him that was the reason they couldn't get presents.

We have been unintentionally programmed by our parents to believe in the scarcity of money. They say things like "There is never enough money! That's just the way it is!" Our traumatic experiences begin around the age of six or seven when we begin to hear our parents make similar complaints and notice the size of the houses we live in, the clothes we wear, and the cars our parents drive. We start to buy into the idea of scarcity too. We begin to compare ourselves to our classmates. If they have more than we do, we think we can't have it now. We suddenly want more. What we have isn't enough.

By the age of ten, we know where our parents rank in society and learn about the "real world." If only we had more money, we could get more goodies, more respect, more love, and of course more friends.

By fifteen, most of us become slaves to money, willing to do just about anything to get more of it. Money even begins to affect our relationships as we start to date someone special and want to shower them with presents.

There are often large financial and social gaps between couples. We feel pressure to take our dates out somewhere nice. We certainly don't want to take them to the wrong restaurant, offend them with a terrible present, or show them just how unworthy we are.

A young woman once complained about her current boyfriend to me, "I deserve more expensive presents. He only gets me cheap stuff. Maybe he's not the one, because I deserve to be with someone who can take care of me."

Many of us have been brainwashed—like that dissatisfied young lady—into believing that having more money means having a better life with more love. We are trained to believe we should work hard to get into a good university to get a better job, and then we should earn as much money as possible. We fail to notice that as we climb this ladder hoping to achieve more in our lives, we actually have much less.

We climb and climb and only begin to notice that something is wrong in our early thirties and forties, when we are neck-deep in debt with our mortgages, car loans, student loans, and credit card balances that just won't disappear. Then our children reach the age where they want to go to the best universities, and the hole gets deeper. Suddenly, dreaming about a two-week vacation brings more anxiety than pleasure.

We sense deeply that something is wrong, but we are too busy to stop and think about when the problem started.

WE ARE ALL INFLUENCED BY THE PAST

As I said, most of us have both fun and bitter memories involving money from when we were small.

A seventy-year-old client of mine cried like a baby when he talked about his mom and money. They had had such a hard time when he was young, she couldn't put food on the table all the time, let alone get him a toy for his birthday. Although wealthy and successful now, he can't get comfortable with his wealth. Fear dominates his every thought. His ultimate nightmare is that one day he will lose everything overnight. His memories of his childhood are still so vivid, the trauma continues to haunt him.

He is not the only one.

Everywhere in the world, people have been so hurt by money-related drama, especially when their families were involved.

If you want to be free of money worries, you may need to dig into your past relationship with money and examine what your early traumas were. What are your fears? How and why does money control you? What have you been brainwashed to believe? While it can be painful and somewhat traumatic to look back, by understanding where you are today in regard to your relationship to money and your unconscious beliefs about money, you'll be better able to see how it controls your life. After this process, you will feel much lighter and happier.

Although painful, recognizing the "YOU ARE HERE" mark is a very necessary step in getting you from where you are now to where you want to go.

"Your Money History" (see page 127) shows how to identify your own personal patterns with money and what kind of relationship you have had with it up until now. As much as many of us would like to deny it, our parents and grandparents were responsible for most of the beliefs about money that we have absorbed. All of this together creates a money blueprint. However, once you look back on your history and see where you came from, you can rewrite this blueprint in order to take you where you really want to go, and choose which beliefs to keep and which to throw away because they no longer serve you.

MONEY AND EMOTIONS

When we think about money, a lot of different emotions naturally surface. Someone who feels negative emotions in one situation could feel something completely different in another, such as deep appreciation or excitement.

Most of these feelings show up below our level of awareness, so we don't actually spend time consciously thinking about what we feel.

But when we experience these feelings only at a sub-conscious level, we are unintentionally limiting the way we experience our life. Without your even noticing, worry or anxiety that you experience because of money—especially when it is vague and hard to detect—can take over and overshadow your life.

For instance, perhaps there is something you really wanted to do for yourself or someone else, but because of anxiety about how to pay for it, you ended up choosing not to do anything at all. Or perhaps you are currently choosing to stay at a job that you know doesn't suit you. Or maybe you have uncontrolled outbursts: you get upset over sudden or unexpected expenses you weren't prepared for and end up criticizing your significant other for something unrelated. These are just a few examples of how we can easily be affected by our feelings about money at any point in time.

Over many years as a consultant, I have seen firsthand what kinds of feelings people experience when money is involved. Like the wealthy old man who cried over his mother being unable to buy him a toy, many of my clients would be brought to tears when discussing childhood memories related to money. Others acted out in different ways. They were petty and impetuous. They would be quick to complain or even sue someone over trivial matters because they were so upset and desperate about their current life situations. Our feelings about money can reach deep places inside us that aren't normally accessible in other circumstances.

HAPPY MONEY

Perhaps that is why money is one of the top reasons couples divorce. If you look into it a little, you might even see that money is quite often the source of frustration in your relationships or business problems.

I'd like to have you do a bit of a self-assessment to see what emotions you most commonly experience when you think about or deal with money. I'll go through some of the most common emotions and you can see which apply best to your life. Once you understand the kinds of feelings you have about money, the amount of stress you feel because of money will drop substantially. Why? Because we can't fix or work on what we don't know. Through self-awareness and observation, we can ameliorate our moods and relationships. We can begin to reframe our approaches to money. We can stop seeing it as something that harms us and begin to see it as something that has the potential to bring good into our lives.

So let's get started.

THE MANY EMOTIONS THAT MONEY PROVOKES IN YOU

There are more emotions than the ones below, of course, but I've selected some of the most prevalent that I have witnessed. There are no "right" ones to have, but some will have either positive or negative effects on your life and well-being.

1. Anxiety and Fear

When people spend money, they often experience some level of anxiety. As they take out their cash or credit card to hand to a cashier, they worry about whether they have made the right choice.

Another common feeling is worrying about what would happen if the money you have right now ran out. Would you end up homeless if you suddenly lost your job? Some people fear just getting through the week, living from paycheck to paycheck. *What if I can't feed my kids this week?* Fear and anxiety about money dominate most people's daily lives. It is why so many people stay in horrible jobs, decrepit houses, bad neighborhoods, or abusive relationships. Often people on the outside looking in say things like "Why do you stay?" or "Why do you put up with it?" The short answer is fear: Fear of the unknown. Fear of what will happen if they make a change. Fear that they don't have the strength or wherewithal to make the move. But they will offer an oft-used excuse: "I don't have enough money to make the moves I need to." So they stay. But it is important to remember that whatever fears you experience about your life and the future don't really have *a direct* relationship to money itself. What do I mean by that? I mean that fears related to money are a result of other unconscious fears.

You don't just fear not having enough money to provide for yourself; *you have fear of failure.* You may have fears of being inadequate in the eyes of your parents or loved ones or community. The fears you have about not being worthy, deserving, or good enough could very well be manifesting themselves in your relationship to money. You may think: *If only I had more money, I'd be more deserving of someone's love. If only I made more money, I'd be valued by my colleagues and friends.* So you strive for more and more. Meanwhile, your anxiety around money builds and builds. Unless you stop and actually confront the inner fears and the self-limiting thoughts that you have about yourself, it won't matter how you try to deal with your money problems, because the core of the issue will still remain untouched.

2. Anger and Resentment

It's not hard to find someone who feels anger or resentment about money. When we feel we didn't get paid as promised, we feel angry. When there is a shortage of money, we get upset easily. When we see that others have more than we do or earn more than we do, we start to feel that we are being shortchanged somehow. Sometimes we get angry at people who we think are the cause of our money problems.

So many crimes occur because of these emotions. Why? Because money is linked so closely with our survival. With the exception of a few tribes left on earth, we all need money to exchange for food, clothing, shelter, and health care. Without money, we die. Our kids die. Yes, the stakes are high. So when we don't get what we believe we deserve or what we have earned—or if we feel robbed or taken advantage of—we feel threatened. That is to say, our lives feel threatened. And what do our brains do when they feel threatened? Thanks to the amygdala in our brain, we have a fight-or-flight response mechanism that takes over to help us survive in these life-threatening situations. While some of us do run in these circumstances, most of us fight. We get angry. We become enraged. *It's not fair! I want my money! Now!* However, the reality is that most of us aren't in real, immediate danger of dying. A bear isn't chasing us through the woods and a shark isn't attacking us (although it can feel like that when we are panicked about money). Nevertheless, we are so often in fight-or-flight mode—fighting for this idea of survival—that we don't see there is a better way to manage our emotions. And in our modern world, the key to happiness is recognizing that we don't need to constantly fight; we don't need to be angry or resentful.

3. Sadness and Sorrow

When we remember our childhoods and think of the dreams we had for ourselves, then look at our current lives, which don't seem to match our youthful fantasies, it's natural to feel a little let down, disappointed, and sad. Who hasn't experienced that feeling? A dream that didn't come true can be truly heartbreaking. And it's not just our own hopes and dreams we mourn. We want to give so much to our kids or our families, and when we can't because of our limited resources, we get down on ourselves. Then we look out at the world full of tragedies—corruption, war, death, and senseless horrors—and we think: *This is all because of money.* Our collective sorrow about injustice, pain, suffering, and heartbreaking loss can be debilitating if left unmanaged.

4. Hatred and Desperation

If you are taken advantage of, you may feel a general sense of outrage, but at some point you begin to feel hatred toward the person or entity that did this to you. If you feel the situation cannot be changed, you begin to turn that hatred inward—toward yourself—and become desperate or depressed. We have all witnessed a couple fighting through a bitter divorce. One party always feels wronged, cut out, or taken advantage of. The anger that grew out of being threatened or harmed in some way turns into hatred. Some feel hatred toward the offending party; others turn that hatred inward and become so forlorn and depressed, they feel helpless to change their circumstances. Divorce, layoffs, salary cuts, diminished returns, or threats of losing one's home all cause these responses. Remember the man who went to my father asking for assistance? He was desperate, filled with self-loathing and hatred, and he ultimately committed suicide. Violent crime, suicide, depression, and hopeless despair can all happen when our anger is fixated on someone else or ourselves.

5. Superiority and Inferiority

I would go so far as to say these are the primary emotions that drive us to buy most of the things we actually don't need. Have you ever bought something because you didn't want the salesperson to think you were stingy or had bad taste? Have you ever bought an extravagant gift you couldn't afford because you wanted to impress a friend? Face it, we have all bought something because we felt obliged to in order to avoid appearing stingy or poor. Or we may buy things so we look better than others. The world is full of "brand names." Otherwise rational humans actually *pay extra money to advertise expensive goods for someone else*! We think it is a badge of honor to spend more money on something. Who really needs a mega-mansion with ten bedrooms or twelve bathrooms and a five-car garage for a family of four? Who really needs to own thirty jackets or a hundred pairs of designer shoes? The answer is obviously "no one." So why do we do it? We spend money so we don't have to feel inferior in front of others or so we can feel superior to those around us. It's that simple. That is why members of the upper middle class are constantly struggling to buy expensive brands to look wealthier than they really are. They don't want to feel inferior to their more affluent friends, and they want to feel superior to those lower-middle-class folks they are trying desperately to separate themselves from. Unless they are into fashion as a hobby or appreciate it as an art form, truly wealthy people don't necessarily feel the need to buy famous brands for the sake of looking good. They don't need a brand name to stake their claim. Warren Buffett, one of the wealthiest men in the world, lives in the same home that he and his wife bought in 1958 for a little over $31,000. It's estimated that its current value is only 0.001 percent of his total net worth. Most of us live in houses that far exceed our means because we care so much about what others think of us versus what we actually truly need to live happy, comfortable lives. When asked why he still lives in the modest home and hasn't upgraded to a more extravagant residence, which he can obviously afford, Buffett told BBC News, "I'm happy there." Translation: He's present there. He has no anxiety about the future, no anger about the past. He is happy because he is free from time and illusions of scarcity.

6. Guilt and Shame

Wealthy people often suffer from feelings of guilt, especially if they inherited money from relatives. Although they may not feel guilt toward someone specific, it can be a general malaise that overwhelms them. Some rich people spend their entire lives feeling embarrassed by their wealth or burdened by the expectations that people have of them and their money. They see others in the world working so hard for so little, and their guilt is reinforced. People in this situation can be more prone to drug or alcohol abuse in order to numb these feelings.

If guilt is something that rich people feel for having too much, shame is the emotion that some people feel when they are struggling financially. Even in childhood people can feel shame for not having enough. Not being able to afford things that other people have can make a person believe that they are somehow flawed. When this feeling persists, it can drive people to work harder rather than smarter and deprive them of the joy in life that anyone deserves to have, regardless of their income.

7. Numbness

This is actually common among all of us. We don't like to feel much in our daily lives. Feeling things requires some sort of action or reaction; most of us don't want to take the necessary actions to manage the feelings appropriately, so we numb ourselves as much as possible—whether it's with food, alcohol, drugs, television, or just "checking out" and going through the motions. So we go for "numb." Many of us try to numb our feelings especially when it comes to money. We don't want to feel "affected" by money, so we suppress our true feelings—whether those emotions are anxiety or elation. For example, I remember an experiment that some television program was airing. They set up cameras to record the facial expressions of consumers when they were checking out with their items. The higher the price at checkout, the less expressive the consumer was. Maybe they were trying to hide the joy and pride that they had felt while shopping. Maybe they were ashamed or embarrassed by such a large purchase. Or perhaps they were trying to avoid unnecessary attention or jealousy. Depending on their relationship with money and the beliefs they have about what money means to them, people's emotions may vary. But somehow and for some reason we've been trained not to express these emotions in public, out of fear of either ridicule or jealousy. However, in our attempts to suppress and numb our emotions to avoid unwanted attention, we invariably suppress positive emotions as well.

8. Excitement and Joy

Kids can show excitement and joy more freely than adults. Just head down to your nearest playground and watch kids run around and play. They celebrate each other, clapping and jumping up and down when someone else does something cool or amazing. They laugh freely at themselves and others. There isn't a hint of self-consciousness or worry. They're there to have fun and they know it. Adults can feel this way, too, on occasion, but it's typically not socially acceptable to jump up and clap or dance with joy when we're excited in our normal, everyday lives, especially when it pertains to money. Can you imagine an employee who jumps up and claps on receiving news of a raise? *We're grown-ups! We don't do that!* Can you imagine joyfully shouting out when you receive an unexpected gift or buy something for yourself that you've always wanted?

KEN HONDA

Joy and happiness are the positive feelings that money can bring to us. But we've been trained or conditioned not to gush about these things. *When was the last time you were so excited about money?* What if I told you that if you allowed yourself to feel the joy of receiving money and spending money, you would likely invite more into your life? For a lot of people this is a concept that's hard to comprehend. They were simply told over and over that money doesn't buy happiness. True, it can't buy "happiness"—which we know comes from within and being present—but it can bring you feelings of joy and gratitude, and, yes, it can make you feel "happy."

9. Appreciation and Love

When our friends or family members give us presents, it's quite natural to feel appreciated and loved. That is why sometimes the energy attached to money feels so much like love. Many of us literally show love with money. We buy gifts that feel meaningful. We want to help alleviate others' stress or concerns. Getting a verbal thank-you for something feels great, but when we receive money or gifts from the people around us for doing something, we feel even more appreciated or validated. In fact, when someone graciously buys us something or gives us something, we feel honored and accepted. We feel *valued*. At work, if your clients and customers are very happy with your performance and are willing to pay more, it makes not only you, the recipient of the money, happy; it makes the givers happy too. They are putting their money into something—or more accurately someone—who brings them joy, happiness, and peace. Even if the gifts or amounts are small, if they are given with love, appreciation, and joy, the recipient can literally feel that energy.

Investments can be a form of love too. The British band Mumford & Sons has a song with the lyric "Where you invest your love, you invest your life." When we invest our money in things we love and care about, we give ourselves and others that loving energy. I often ask my audience to name the biggest gift they ever received from someone *not* in their own families. I usually see a lot of hands go up in the group. Some say $10,000 or $50,000. The biggest number I ever heard was $500,000! A happy customer gifted a sushi chef with this amount of money! Can you imagine? Apparently the chef had mentioned wanting to have his own restaurant someday and told his customer that he was saving $100 a month from his salary. After hearing the story, the customer commented that it would take years to do it, and the chef explained that he had already been saving for ten years and still didn't have enough. The customer replied that he would fund the chef's restaurant and would do it within two years. But the chef hesitated, saying, "I don't have any collateral!" The customer replied, "That's okay. I am impressed with your attitude and want to support you. *I love you and love what you do.*" That customer put loving energy behind his money and invested it in someone he cared about. It not only made the chef feel loved; it confirmed what he loved in the process.

10. Happiness

We all feel happy when we receive an unexpected bonus or a surprise influx of cash. It could be a gift from our parents or in the form of a tax refund. *We simply feel happy.* What do I mean by "happy"? I mean we can be present, without worrying about the future or having anxiety about the past, because we finally feel we have enough for the time being. We can breathe a sigh of relief. We also feel that with more money we have more choices.

But what if I told you it was possible to feel happy before the money even came to you? What if you could look at all you have and say, "It's enough"? If you believe it's enough—I mean, truly believe it—then I guarantee you'll feel happy . . . so happy, in fact, that surprising things may just happen. Things will work out as they need to. It doesn't matter if you're Warren Buffett or Jimmy Buffett or if you can only afford the $9.99 all-you-can-eat buffet: if you think you have enough, you will be happy. Yes, it is possible to have a happy mind-set and emotions when it comes to money. It comes from inside—before the money even flows your way. If you, too, want to feel this, simply focus on that happy, contented feeling. Believe that you have more than enough, and if you need more, it will come from somewhere.

WHY IS IT SO HARD TO HAVE A
HAPPY RELATIONSHIP WITH MONEY?

Most people have a difficult relationship with money because the ways they earn and spend it are unhealthy. Which is to say, a lot of people work at a job they hate just for the paycheck, and the stress adds up quickly. Suffering is embedded in the act of getting money. Without realizing it, feelings of stress, pain, or irritation come up every time they use or think about money. Even though those feelings originated from doing the work they dislike, the lines between work and money are blurred. When you force yourself to earn money at a job you hate doing in the first place, it becomes that much harder to let that money go without a damn good reason. You feel the pressure not to waste it. In fact, it irritates you to spend a dime on anything. When money feels hard to come by, it's definitely harder to let go of it. It's also ingrained in us by our parents in our childhood that we should never waste money. Those memories pop up quietly in the form of stress, telling us not to spend more than necessary whenever possible. That leaves us constantly looking at how much we have left and then worrying over how to save or earn more! We end up feeling a lot more confused than we need to be. Whenever money is involved, we have this tendency to fret over how to spend it or think we may have made the wrong choices. We feel frustrated earning money, excited when spending it, then worried about whether it will be there in the future. Eventually we get fed up with this pattern and wish for a world without money at all. (Careful what you wish for! The law of attraction will help you realize that dream, at least as far as your own bank account!)

So what about the happy, prosperous people we sometimes hear about? They're like unicorns! We've heard of them, but most of us rarely interact with them. But I assure you they are out there, and their relationship with money is completely different in every way. They earn money doing things that bring them joy—and that joy begets joy. It brings with it fun, excitement, and gratitude. When they spend money, they also feel happiness or appreciation. So stress is not a part of the equation at all.

They carry a quiet confidence in their ability to earn or come up with money when needed, so they don't feel much stress or anxiety about the future either. When it comes to money, this type of person acts almost entirely out of positive emotions. That's the biggest difference between happy, prosperous people and the type I mentioned before.

SO WHY ARE WE SO AFRAID?

The reason why we are so afraid is that we have been hurt by money in the past. Some of us learned at a young age to have few expectations when it came to money: You wanted something badly for your birthday or Christmas and you didn't get that exact present. Or maybe you were scolded for spending too much or too quickly after receiving money as a gift. Or you were a poor student and your parents struggled to pay your tuition, so they yelled at you for wasting their hard-earned money. Or perhaps your spouse blamed you for a "bad decision" you made with money. Spouses often have very different ideas of how and when money should be spent. Arguments erupt and fingers get pointed. And in the end everyone is left with negative feelings about money. Instead of understanding their attitudes toward money, people blame money—or more often their lack of it—for being the problem. I've watched parents berate their children for choosing expensive birthday gifts for their friends instead of congratulating their children on their openness and generosity. If more parents had a healthy relationship with money, they would praise their children first and then teach them about money and the appropriate amount to spend on a gift. We receive so many proverbial punches in the gut when we are young that we begin to think that any kind of spending is bad. Whatever we do is not "right." And soon this translates into: *Whatever we do, it will not be enough.* So when we make money decisions, we act out of fear instead of love.

What are we afraid of? Doing something wrong. We fear we're paying too much. We doubt our own decisions—so much so, we can't make the most basic buying decision, whether we're purchasing a bag of coffee or a car. We instantly doubt it. Then, because we already don't feel great about it, we regret it. Then come the complaints and neg-ative thoughts about money: *I got a bad deal. Nothing ever works out for me. Money goes out faster than it comes in. I'll never have enough at this rate. I'm so stupid.* Sound familiar? You're not alone. Lots of people think like this and behave like this, because it's all they've ever been taught.

SOME NEGATIVE BELIEFS ABOUT MONEY THAT MAY BE HOLDING YOU BACK

One of my clients held the belief that money wouldn't stay with her. Even though she made good money, she could not keep it. It was a self-fulfilling prophecy. We manifest what we believe in life. However, most of us aren't even aware of the many negative subconscious beliefs that we've been operating under for years. I will share with you many of the negative and positive beliefs that have been encoded in our blueprints and passed down from generation to generation. As you go over these negative beliefs, I invite you to examine which ones you may hold—in fact, you may even shout out, as some of my clients do: "This one! That is exactly what I believe!"

Let's start with negative beliefs.

Money is bad. A lot of people have a negative view of money. At the very least, they feel they have to be cautious when they deal with money. Whatever you do, you have to be careful. Money can be a bad thing.

Money disappears fast. When you need money most, you cannot find it. It quickly disappears. Right after it comes into your life, it will go fast! In Japanese we used to call it *oashi*, which means "feet." Money seems to walk quickly away from you. I guess we can all relate a little to this one!

Money hurts people. This is also a common belief. Money, in the literal sense, cannot hurt people. However, we may feel hurt because money triggers some pain in us: sometimes it triggers our lack of self-worth, sometimes our past relationship issues. Sometimes people do use money as a weapon. They use it to attack others or buy things that can cause harm to people.

Money is scary. When we think that money can accomplish anything, money seems bigger than what it is. We know we can get hurt by money. That is why we begin to be afraid of money. We are afraid of many things. But money by itself is not scary.

Money creates trouble. If you have a bad memory about money, you may feel this way. But money doesn't create trouble; *we* do. We create trouble when we break promises or contracts, withhold money out of greed, miss payments, or don't use it in a sincere way.

Money invites jealousy. We are afraid of negative attention in general. Having a lot of money can cause that. So if you feel hesitant about having a lot of money for this reason, that is understandable too.

Now here are some positive beliefs about money:

Money supports people. Of course, money can support people by enabling them to make a living, helping them learn new things, and providing them with security and all the necessities required to live.

Money makes people happy. As I mentioned in previous sections, money does elicit positive emotions as well. You can in fact feel happy about money even if you have only a little of it. When given or received with happy energy, money can make someone feel good. Even a postcard can make someone feel happy.

Money helps realize dreams. This is a good one too. People have all kinds of dreams, and sometimes money helps to fund them. They can be as expensive as a trip to Mars or they can cost very little.

Money bonds people. If you spend money wisely, you can help create better relationships. For example, you can use money to plan a family trip and make happy memories that will last a lifetime. You can use money to make all kinds of fun arrangements that bring you closer to your family and friends. Sometimes I use my money to treat young students to lunch. I'll invite twenty or thirty together and we'll talk and laugh.

Money warms people's hearts. You can send flowers to sick friends. You can send money to foster care facilities. A few years ago, there was an anonymous donation of school backpacks to a local orphanage here in Japan. The sender of the gift called him- or herself "Tigermask," which is the name of a famous cartoon character in Japan. After news of the donation was broadcast on TV, hundreds of similar donations started to arrive not only at the orphanage but at nursing homes and other places that needed similar support. That movement inspired everyone and gave them a warm feeling.

YOUR MONEY HISTORY

Your money history is how you have lived with money.

Since you were small, how has your relationship with money been? Is it a happy one or a frustrated one? When you think of the past, does that give you nice feelings or make you feel tense?

As we have discussed in previous sections, it's clear that there are many misunderstandings we humans have about money. If you recall significant events that took place and investigate what really happened, you know the truth. It is often liberating.

As we know, we have been heavily influenced by our parents with regard to money. If our parents had a healthy relationship with money, our financial life is probably pretty good. But most of our parents were damaged one way or another when it came to money, so chances are most of us are pretty damaged too. You won't have to dig too hard to remember your parents fighting about money. Probably the memories are still pretty fresh. Those ugly fights seem to stick with us for some reason. You may have seen your mom and dad very upset with each other or with you and your siblings. Your parents might have fought about spending too much or earning too little—or maybe they blamed each other or their kids for the fact that there was never enough. Someone always had to be at fault. No matter what the fights were about, recalling them has the power to stir up even the most suppressed feelings. If you had a single parent, they may not have had anyone to argue with, but they may have taken their angst out on you or their other children. You may have observed your mother or father worrying about financial matters. If your parents ever got physical or violent, or at the very least loud and aggressive when arguing, you, too, could be aggressive about money with people, even the ones you care deeply about.

Most of us have several negative memories involving money. But even those of us with the worst of childhoods can recall some good moments with money. Perhaps you once *did* receive something you asked for. Maybe one of your relatives surprised you with cash. Or maybe you were granted permission to see a movie with friends and were given a few dollars to go.

All the memories, both good and bad, add up in your head and form a belief that money is a certain thing. For some people, money can create so many happy things. For others, money can cause pain and confusion in the family. It can be the source of anger, angst, and agony.

The beliefs that were created in our childhoods are usually hidden deep within our psyches. They influence how we deal with money at the most basic level. When we earn and spend money, we do it based on rules that may not make much sense. Nevertheless, we abide by these subconscious rules because we don't know how to operate any other way. And we do it at our own peril.

These beliefs also surface when we have to make decisions in our careers and relationships. We may choose stability over excitement because of our deeply ingrained money worries. We may choose a partner based solely on his or her financial status rather than love.

It is sad that this process is so automatic, and we don't even realize that it is happening—that it affects so much of our lives, our dreams, our jobs, and, perhaps most concerning, our relationships with our loved ones. For example, one of my clients was upset at her husband because he was buying a cheap gift for a wedding they were attending. She was ashamed and embarrassed. This was clearly going against her beliefs. So she told him that it was shameful and cheap to send such a gift. However, in his family it was shameful to waste, to spend more than was deemed necessary. Because of their contrasting beliefs, they fought. And of course both thought that they were right. But nobody was right. It is simply that there are many ways to deal with money. Everyone has their own beliefs and approach. And often, this is the source of most conflicts relating to money. However, if we recognized that *there is no right way* and tried to understand where our spouse or partner was coming from, we would not suffer so much, and I believe most divorces could be avoided.

YOUR CURRENT FINANCIAL SITUATION AND YOUR FAMILY HISTORY

Your financial situation is deeply connected with your family history. As I said before, we are taught by our parents about life. However, we didn't learn our lessons about money from them the way we learned our lessons at school. Instead we absorbed the lessons: everything we saw, heard, and felt from a very young age stuck with us. Perhaps you heard yelling and screaming over money, so you learned that you should yell and scream about money as well. Your parents looked grumpy when they paid the bills, and now you look grumpy when you pay yours. What we don't realize is that every behavior, both good and bad, comes primarily from the learned behaviors we witnessed as young children. Without being conscious of why we do what we do, we can't change what we do. And sometimes we have to go far back in our family trees to find the roots of our financial issues.

Your Grandparents

If we're influenced by our parents, it's not hard to guess where they learned their behaviors and attitudes toward money: *their* parents!

If you truly want to understand the intricacies of your relationship with money, my advice is to seek out both sets of grandparents. Our parents give us just a piece of the whole puzzle. But they had four very different people influencing them, both in their childhoods and, in many cases, early in their marriages. Surprisingly, most of us don't bother to ask our parents, let alone our grandparents, about their childhoods, their struggles, or their successes. We may just know their occupations—that they were teachers, policemen, engineers, doctors, or lawyers—but we don't know who they really are. We rarely dig deeper to find out what motivated them when they were young, how they felt about things—namely, what they were most proud of or what they worried about.

Without us consciously knowing it, our deepest fears are in fact our grandparents' fears. Unless we examine what they experienced closely and come to terms with their experiences, we can't really know why we believe what we do regarding money. If your grandparents have passed away, I suggest reading general histories of their eras or asking some

of their contemporaries—perhaps aged aunts and uncles—
what they were like and how they survived during difficult
times. I researched my own grandparents and discovered
a treasure trove. It wasn't a coincidence that I followed my
father into business. One of my grandfathers was also a
very successful businessman and died at forty-two, but in
my research I discovered he was more of a "gambler." He
used to buy ships full of merchandise and fish with cash
and then turn around and sell them for a massive profit.
While he was successful and made money happily this way,
his son—my father—wanted to be seen as a legitimate
businessman and wanted to be respected by his peers, so he
went into accounting and finance. So much of my father's
personality and relationship with money makes more sense
in light of this information about my grandfather's past. Very
often we don't realize the extent to which our relationships
with money are connected with our grandparents and consequently *our* parents. Coming to terms with this can be
powerfully transformative. Once we know why we think the
way we do about money, we can begin to heal and change.

Siblings and Close Friends

Parents and grandparents are not the only ones who impact
the way we unconsciously see the world. Our siblings,
friends, and larger peer group also influence our behaviors
and beliefs. I once had a classmate who taught me the bad
habit of buying junk food after school. He was somewhat

of a rebel. Buying food after school without our parents' permission was strictly forbidden, and because it was, it was all the more fun! I wouldn't have thought to do that on my own, but friends can hold powerful sway over what we deem cool, fun, or worth our time and money. We watch everyone around us during these formative years, pick up others' habits, and layer them into our own.

By the time we're young adults, we're carrying a lot of messed-up beliefs, behaviors, and attitudes about money, and we have little awareness about how much we truly can take control of them. We don't realize just how much damage has been done to us, and unless we seek ways to heal the damage, we will remain a mess—and so will our finances.

YOUR FORGOTTEN SCARS: REMEMBERING YOUR HURT FEELINGS

It is amazing how forgetful we are regarding what happened in our childhoods. People often forget what they went through. A lot of abused children think they had great childhoods. Families often brainwash their children, saying things like "Oh, you had it easy," or "You have it so good," or "We had such a wonderful family back then." Some families collectively buy into the lie. Siblings will sit around and wax poetic about their parents or their childhoods. Somehow they forget the struggles—or, rather, they try to gloss over them—because remembering them is painful or makes them uncomfortable.

I was definitely one of those kids who grew up thinking my childhood was "okay." I told myself that story for a long time, because the alternative—remembering the painful parts of my past—didn't make me feel great. But as I allowed myself to remember my hidden wounds and scars, I realized my childhood was far from okay.

In fact, it was pretty terrible. Money—or the fear of discussing money—dominated my mother's life and therefore my youth. I remember once asking her to send me to a summer camp that I badly wanted to attend, but because she was afraid of bringing up the subject to my father—who would often get upset about what he deemed unnecessary expenses—she didn't ask. Instead she advised that we wait until my father was in a good mood. Translation: *Never.* I was forbidden to talk about my request even at the kitchen table. Due to my fear of angering my father, that dream (and others) crashed and burned before I could even get up the courage to ask for help in pursuing it. When I was older, I realized that I often kept silent about my dreams, primarily to protect my mom from my dad's abuse. And he was abusive. That was a terrible and painful fact of my childhood. His anger could be triggered by the slightest thing: something that upset him—something as innocuous as a child's request to go to summer camp—would set him off. Children often remember their parents' favorite catchphrases; well, my mother's catchphrases were revealing. They weren't anything like "Do your best!" or "Just have fun!" or "You can do anything you put your mind to!" Instead the advice my mother passed on to me was:

"Don't wake a sleeping baby."

"Don't make a noise."

"Let's wait for Dad to be in a good mood."

For a long time, I was haunted by this. In Japan it is taboo to speak of one's family drama or pain. It's taboo to talk in such a way about hardworking fathers who provide for their families, but the reality was that my hardworking father passed on to his son a lot of damaging beliefs and ideas about money.

It wasn't easy for me to undo a lot of the negative thinking and fear that had been instilled in me. The only way I could do that was if I was willing to admit that those fears and beliefs were there in the first place.

Remembering your childhood trauma and incidents can be tough, but if you're committed to changing your relationship with money, it's a necessary step.

SO HOW DO YOU HEAL YOUR MONEY WOUNDS?

Our bodies and minds seem to remember past hurts. Whether something happened in the distant past or more recently, we feel the wound acutely when a new experience reopens it. It doesn't matter how much mental scar tissue we've managed to form: when someone threatens to take something we have or desire—such as money—we react in the same way we did as children. We feel deeply hurt.

We feel worthless or somehow not deserving. For some reason we human beings instinctually equate our self-worth with our ability to get things or achieve things. If we receive good grades, accolades, or even presents, our presence on this planet seems validated. If good grades, compliments, or presents are withheld from us, we somehow take this very personally. Something must be wrong with us. Something must be terribly wrong. Then we look outward and compare ourselves with others. So-and-so got the toy we wanted. So-and-so got the achievement award. These people are somehow worthier, better, more deserving. We learn at a very young age that who we are and our inherent value as human beings is deeply connected to what we can achieve or get. As we grow up, the same rules apply. If we receive a promotion, get a raise, or are showered with gifts and accolades, our worthiness as human beings is confirmed.

In reality, though, we know that there is actually no connection between one's financial situation and one's inherent worth as a human being. Nevertheless, people believe this because this is all they have been taught their entire lives.

One way to heal your past financial wounds is to accept that what you learned is not your fault, and it's not your parents' fault. They learned from their parents, who learned from theirs. Collectively, as a society, we all share some responsibility for perpetuating these beliefs. We affirm them often and regularly. So when people don't have money, or they can't give money away or do things they want to do because they don't have enough money, they feel worthless. They feel powerless. And what do people who feel powerless and worthless do? They yell. They scream. They take it out on their kids. Take a moment and go back in time and try to remember a time you heard your parents yell at you about money. Or perhaps they told you that you couldn't do something you really wanted to do because they didn't have enough money. Maybe you're crying in your memory, because it meant you had to give up a lifelong dream—perhaps to go to college or travel overseas.

This is where the healing takes place. And the healing comes from understanding and forgiveness. I want you to go back to that memory and observe your mom or dad in that moment. Do they look like they are in as much pain as you are? Is their anger or demeanor belying the fear and anxiety they have—or perhaps is it masking the disappointment they have in themselves for letting you down? Do you feel for them? Do you have any compassion for them or understand now that they were simply doing the best they could, when they could—that they, too, were carrying around deep wounds about money?

When you try to understand, you can empathize, and ultimately you can forgive and move on. And you can also, most powerfully, forgive yourself. You can forgive yourself for not knowing better in the past, and you can take the necessary steps forward in the future.

CREATING YOUR BEST FUTURE
BY APPRECIATING YOUR PAST

A practice we have here in Japan is that we thank our ancestors regularly. The idea is that when you become conscious and aware of all the work that was done before you, you are more likely to be grateful for what you have. In addition, by linking yourself to your past, you can see the large network of energy that made your life possible today. Many people have no idea how many struggles were overcome to get them where they are today. And once you are able to see yourself in the vast continuum—in the past and future—you're more likely to behave and act with a sense of responsibility for future generations. In addition, you're more aware of the continuum in the present—that your actions affect not only you but everyone around you. And that everything you have comes from a vast network of humans and their collective energy as well. When you eat a piece of lettuce, for example, you're able to see that it was prepared by someone, and before that it was stocked in a store by someone, and before that it was transported in a truck by someone, and before that it was tended, grown, and picked by someone. Once you see that you are just a part of a long, wide, vast network of humanity, then it's easy to be grateful. It's easy to feel a sense of abundance. It's easy to marvel at what you have, even if it's just a piece of lettuce. And that sense of gratitude for the little things can expand exponentially outward with each realization of connectivity to the past, the future, and the present.

After investigating your past and coming to terms with it, you may feel more comfortable and a bit more open to healing and changing your patterns of behavior in the future. (If you already feel pretty happy about the past, you might find it easier to project a nicer future.) So much of our future outlook is dependent on our present or our current beliefs and attitudes. If you can cultivate an appreciation for your hardships and glean important lessons from them, then you're likely to keep a positive attitude when difficult times come again in the future. This is all to say that you and you alone can create your own future, largely by how you think about and act in the present.

The energy that we put out into the world, our beliefs and words and attitudes, is the energy that comes back to us.

CHAPTER 4

The Flow of Money

HAPPY MONEY FLOW, UNHAPPY MONEY FLOW

We already spoke of this earlier—that many of us have a very narrow understanding of what money is, and believe there is a direct correlation between money and the paper and coins we sometimes use. But since we've been using credit cards for most transactions for decades, and now use even smartphones to make purchases, we know that is not true anymore. We don't need cash to make purchases; nevertheless, money seems to flow seamlessly from our accounts to someone else's.

So what is money?

Where does it come from?

Where does it get its value?

In chapters 1 through 3, we looked at money from different angles, but primarily that of what it *means to you*—and your relationship to it insofar as how you regard it and how you have come to feel about it through your own experiences and your past.

In this chapter I am going to ask you to stretch your mind even more. I want you to look at money as *energy* that is flowing all around—most notably among people. When we use money nowadays, it doesn't change hands literally; rather, it changes hands figuratively. You buy something and you pay for it. Whom do you pay this money to? The person whom you are buying from, of course. But whether or not you can see this person is beside the point. Whether you're buying something online or in person, your money is a source of exchange—a current, if you will. Hence the term "currency."

If money is energy and is in constant flow, then it is currently flowing all around us right now in our homes, our communities, and our social circles. It's everywhere. Even if you can't see it, it is there. This may be a new concept and difficult to grasp, but I am sure you will see things differently after this.

In the city, you can feel a certain energy all around you. Why? Because money is flowing rapidly and in abundance. People are buying gas for their cars, they are running to the store for food, they're headed out to do something fun like watch a ball game or see a movie. Everything requires money—and millions of city folks are using it to exchange for goods or services. Meanwhile, in the country you don't feel the same level of energy. Why? Giant expanses of space exist between people and entities where one can spend money, and the energy is diffused and lessened. If it just feels "different" to you in the country, it's not your imagination. Or if you feel different around wealthy people, or wonder why all wealthy people seem to hang out only with other wealthy people, the answer is: they are operating in the same flow—at the same speed, with the same mass.

So how do you get a piece of Happy Money? Or the high-energy, fast-flowing, large mass of money that is flowing around those circles? And how do you avoid Unhappy Money—the low-energy, slow-moving, lower-mass kind of money?

I am going to show you how. It may feel impossible right now, and you may feel a bit lost, but just bear with me and keep thinking of money as flow—as energy, not as cash in hand—and this may be an easier concept to relate to.

What I am going to say here may shock you a bit, but I am not the only one who thinks this way. There are many experts and people who have gone before me who also think what I am about to tell you:

You are responsible for the charge of energy you infuse your money with.

You can quite literally "charge" your money (mass) and flow (speed) with your intensity of energy. If you charge your energy positively, i.e., increase the level of energy associated with money, you will then see an increase in money and flow. It's the law of the universe.

So how do you positively charge your money to create Happy Money? Gratitude and appreciation.

Yes, it's that simple.

HAPPY MONEY FLOW

You can increase your flow of Happy Money simply by showing gratitude and appreciation. When you get paid for a job well done, accept it with sincere appreciation. It will feel as though the money is flowing at an even faster rate. The same goes if the people who work with you—whether your boss, your colleagues, or your employees—all appreciate you as well. When your work is valued, you "matter." And what does matter equal? Energy! What does positive energy feel like? Happy Money!

When your clients and customers also appreciate you for your work or even for just treating them with a professional attitude, you are in a positively charged flow of Happy Money.

When you feel joy toward the work you do, and proud to work with your colleagues and clients, and thank them generously for letting you work with them, you're positively charging your Happy Money flow. When it is your supreme honor to work with others, you are positively charging the Happy Money flow.

And, yes, you can keep charging that flow even when money is going out, not just when it is coming in. If you find the perfect product or service—whether it is clothes, food at a restaurant, or a movie you've just paid to see—and you feel excited and lucky to have found it, you are increasing your positive flow of Happy Money. Whenever you feel joy and excitement for a service or a product, and you show your appreciation, you are sending Happy Money out into the world. When you give your friends money or support a charity that makes a difference or invest in a local start-up that will ultimately help the community or the world, you are increasing the flow of Happy Money—not just in your life but in the lives of others.

FEELING AND OBSERVING THE FLOW OF MONEY

If you take a close look at our world, you can see the flow of money right in front of you (unless, as we established, you live in a remote part of the country).

When I was small, my father took me to a strip mall. He asked me to look in through the entrances of several stores and count how many customers were in each store. He then explained to me what I was witnessing. I had seen many customers in some stores and wrongly assumed, just by how quickly they flowed in and out, that those businesses were more successful or had more money. But my father pointed something out. It's not just the quantity of the flow that counts; it's the price of the purchases that matters as well.

There were many different types of stores, with varying numbers of visitors and goods. The fish store and the vegetable store were the busiest: I saw a constant flow of customers. But I soon realized the customers were coming out with inexpensive items. Then I looked at a mattress store and noticed there weren't as many customers, but I realized that all it would take was one sale and the mattress seller would be able to feed his family for days. Then there was the real estate agency just a few doors down. Selling a home had even bigger returns. If a real estate agent sold just one house, he could live off that sale for months. I learned my lesson that day: *busy doesn't necessarily mean good business.*

That was an eye-opening lesson for a young person, and it stuck with me. When you go inside a shopping mall now, the stores are different, but the rules of money are the same.

Just as an exercise, head out to the nearest mall and sit there and feel the flow of money all around you. Take a look at who is buying and also take note of how many people are coming and going.

If you can feel the energy or the money flow, you will start to see things you have never seen before.

MONEY IS FLOW: MORE IN, MORE OUT

It's easy to recall the ebb and flow of money in your life. Perhaps you remember a time when you had money in the bank and you felt safe and secure. Or perhaps there were times when you had money but you spent more than you made, and consequently felt like you were out of control or filled with dread and fear. Or maybe there were times when you had no money at all and you felt lost or desperate.

"Easy come, easy go," the saying goes.

And it's true: money does come and go. Just as we must eat food to survive, we also have to release it in the form of waste or energy. There must be a flow—a balance, if you will. That is natural law.

And just as we can't control the whims of nature, we cannot intentionally control the flow of money. Just as gravity controls the ebb and flow of the tides, our economy controls the ebb and flow of money. Understanding that money can't just flow constantly toward us should bring you some comfort and appreciation. When it flows in, you should show gratitude, enjoying the feeling as it flows toward you; then, when you invest or spend, you should also release with gratitude and appreciation, knowing that the release can bring just as much joy and, because natural law will take over, that the money will eventually flow back.

FLOW IS NEUTRAL

One of the biggest conundrums regarding the flow of money is who seems to be on the receiving end of it. It's not earth-shattering news to report that immoral, corrupt, unkind, and unscrupulous people can become rich. We can hope that good, kind, and ethical people will become wealthy instead, but the reality is that this is often not the case, as most of us know from personal experience.

So how come seemingly bad people are on the receiving end of so much money?

BECOMING A MONEY MAGNET

My mentor once told me that while money is energy, humans are like magnets. In nature, magnetism is a force, and it is incredibly useful in converting energy from one source to another. Money magnets—those people who seem to be in the direct path of the flow of money—don't have to be morally righteous or ethical to be on the receiving end. Just as nature doesn't discriminate—for example, a rock succumbing to the forces of gravity may fall on a good man or an evil one—money doesn't discriminate either. Good or bad, money doesn't judge. It simply goes where it is pulled. Since humans, companies, and countries are "magnets" or "forces," they have the power to pull the flow toward them. We can cry out "It's not fair!" as much as we want when a corrupt person, institution, or country has more money than we do, but fairness, as you know, also doesn't exist in nature. When I said "It's not fair" to my own mentor, he just smiled and said: "Money is not God. Money is just neutral energy. There are two kinds of magnetic power. Both of them have the same strength. It is the same with partnership. The good ones and bad ones have similar attraction."

Money is similar. Money is energy, and it can be pulled or attracted to magnetic people.

Who are these magnetic people?

Money magnets (the term that is popular to describe very wealthy people) possess a huge desire to make money. They love money. They believe they deserve it. They think about it—and ways to make it, find it, and be next to it. Many had difficult childhoods and found solace in the idea that money would save them. Money would help them right all the injustices in their lives. It's almost as if they developed deep cavities in their hearts and those "black holes" have a powerful magnetic pull. That is why con artists and seemingly bad or unethical people can make and keep making money. However, it is like playing cards with the devil in some ways. As we have said, there is always an ebb and flow with money. So the more they make, the more they stand to lose. Typically, fear of losing money ultimately disrupts their flow. But after they lose it, they desire more and more, and that magnetic pull happens once again. It's an endless cycle.

Conversely, people who hate money seem to repel it. They had tough childhoods, too, but were taught money was the source of all their problems and worries. They wish there were "no such thing as money," so that's exactly what they get.

BECOMING A POSITIVE MAGNET

There is a way, however, for good people to become powerful magnets for the flow of money—and that is by emitting positive energy. People with positive attitudes emit this energy and have an ability to attract money too. Loving what you do and exhibiting a grateful, happy energy exert an incredible pull on the flow of money. Restaurant owners who love cooking and serving their customers attract more people, hence more money. A dry cleaner who has a lot of passion to pull out stains and return clothes to their owners in a timely manner will likely keep and attract many clients. Lawyers who love helping people seek justice will undoubtedly have a line of clients waiting.

People with lots of love, energy, and compassion are naturally attractive and alluring. It's not an accident that we are attracted to genuinely nice people. If given the choice between the flower shop owner who loves flowers and creating beautiful arrangements and someone who does it just because it is her job, whom would you prefer to buy flowers from?

It's really not "magic" that nice, passionate, and enthusiastic people attract customers and therefore money. The result over time is that they will undoubtedly be able to build wealth. Though not necessarily a priority or an aim, making more money can nevertheless be a bonus for loving and serving people.

WHEN MORE MONEY COMES IN THAN GOES OUT

Typically, when more money is coming in than is going out, we feel pretty good about life. And most likely we feel excited about what we do too. At times it can feel overwhelming, but for the most part it's just fun. In fact, this is absolutely the time in our life when we should be enjoying it. All that we've done in the past is flowing back to us as a reward for our hard work and service. It's a clear sign that we're doing what we're supposed to be doing: mainly, serving people and making them happy. This is also the time we should think about investing our money for our future, knowing that it is natural for money to ebb and flow. Some of us may even want to buy new equipment for our work or learn new things, discover new hobbies, and find ways to continue to give back.

However, most people don't take this time to *enjoy* the influx of money or *invest* in themselves or their futures. Rather, they think, *This will go on forever*, and raise their standard of living—and once again find themselves struggling to survive, because they are still living beyond their means. And everyone knows that once you get into the habit of spending more, it's difficult to rein it in. Many even feel societal or familial expectations to keep doing so long after they are unable to: they are expected to entertain, throw parties, and give lavish gifts, because that is what they have always done. However, this proves disastrous when the money flow is low again: *What do you mean, I have to pay taxes? How much will this unexpected medical bill cost?*

WHEN LESS MONEY FLOWS THAN IS REQUIRED

Most of us have been there. And we can say with absolute certainty that this is one of the most terrifying times of our lives. We all know the familiar physical feelings that accompany acute financial distress: the aching and persistent knot in the stomach, the pressure that squeezes like a band around the chest, and the quickening of the heart. Perhaps an important sale falls through and we won't be getting the commission we were hoping for. Perhaps our furnace suddenly goes out and we need (but don't have) the $4,000 to replace it. Or perhaps, like so many others, we're drowning in school loans and credit card debt and just can't seem to get ahead.

Most of us face such issues, but I believe it's *how* we face them that ensures a more positive outcome. No one is exempt from calamity or distress, and stressful situations can be some of our greatest teachers: they tell us what we need and what we desire, but mostly they force us to grow. And, yes, growing sometimes hurts. It's why we call them *growing pains*. And we all are going through them. If you are single and have a modest lifestyle, you probably designed a life in which you need to worry very little about money. Good for you! Keep it up! But chances are, if you're reading this, you've had some stress in your life with regard to money. And I can pretty much guarantee that if you are married and have kids, you feel financial pressure. In fact, it feels like it's *always there*. It's like a pervasive feeling that never goes away. And it seems to increase in intensity as the children grow older. Suddenly the toys kids want become more expensive and their demands increase for big-ticket items: concert tickets, smartphones, computers, headphones, cars, maybe even trips abroad. . . . The list is endless—and expensive. And that doesn't even include the cost of college. It feels like you're always teetering on the edge of absolute ruin or collapse—one lost client, and you could lose your job. One more fight with your spouse about where all the money is going, and divorce seems imminent.

Remember, these situations are temporary. Remind yourself that more income isn't necessarily the answer: as we know, the more people have, the more they tend to spend. Rather, use this time as a period of self-reflection and growth. Realize what you need to do in order to increase the flow of money into your life. (Being grateful for what you *do* have is a start.) Then focus on experiences that make you feel happy, enthusiastic, and positive.

WHEN MORE FLOWS BOTH IN AND OUT

If you have a huge increase in money coming in and going out, then you're feeling pretty confident: you've come through those hard times we just discussed, having learned some essential lessons that you can now use. You're probably expert at managing your expenses and choosing to invest your money in meaningful ways. While growing may have been painful before, now it seems more effortless and painless. And unlike in the previous situation, you now have choices. You can decide to pump the brake and slow down your growth, or push on the gas and accelerate, depending on your own desires and willingness to take risks. If you choose to pump the brake, invariably life will become quieter and more peaceful. But if you're ready to up your game and take your life and your career to the next level, this is the time to do it. Although there is risk, there is usually more fun than trouble to be had.

WHEN THERE IS LITTLE FLOW COMING IN OR OUT

This is what I call "rest mode." Most of us have experienced these times. They typically reflect a lack of action or initiative on our own part. We're not working or we're not reaching out and doing other activities. Why? Some of us could be burned-out after years of exertion, or we could seek to combat stress by taking on more activities or work. There are deep psychological forces at work here. People who don't feel "good enough," "worthy," or "deserving" tend to hide from normal everyday life. Anxiety and fear grip them at every turn. They don't spend money and they don't make money. And it works for them. They don't have to experience the pain of loss, the pain of growth, or the occasional discomfort of failure or disappointment.

If this sounds familiar to you, do you feel that you can keep going this way for the rest of your life?

Do you ever get bored with this lifestyle? If you find yourself uninterested and tired all the time, then this may be a great time to start something—anything—in your life. As you do more, your income and expenses will increase, but so, too, will your human experiences. And yes, some of those experiences will be stressful. If your sole reason for avoiding making or spending money was to avoid stress, then I advise you: Be prepared. Part of life is feeling a bit of stress.

WEALTH HAS TWO PARTS: STOCK AND FLOW

You can categorize wealth in two ways: *stock* and *flow*. Your stock is your collection of savings, stocks, bonds, and real estate. These things help maintain what we call our net worth or our financial value. Some are tangible and others are just numbers in a digital world that can be turned into something else. You can buy food and other goods with assets; assets like stocks, bonds, and properties all generate money as dividends and rent. Other kinds simply "keep value" but may not generate anything unless sold or traded—such as art, classic cars, jewels, and gold.

Flow is your income. If you have assets, you can receive income from them. But if you don't, you need to earn income by working. And life depends on what kind of flow you create. If you create a fun and happy flow, you can feel joy and excitement in everyday life. If you have enough assets, you don't need to worry about work.

When you think of money, it is easy to mix up stock and flow. Most people see money only as flow and therefore never pay much attention to assets.

Working people see their jobs as a source of income. They may think in terms of budgeting—what comes in has to be more than what goes out, but they don't think of "flow" in a critical way—that eventually what flows in will flow out. Without any assurance, many working people automatically expect a steady flow of income—for the rest of their lives. They think, *I have a job, so I am set for life*, and then are surprised when they are laid off or their factory is shut down. If you understand the turbulent nature of flow, then you know it is not guaranteed forever. Once you realize this, you can better prepare yourself for the future. But the reality is that most of us don't. And when we grow up in a family that doesn't teach us this fact but rather "Go to school, go get a job, and you'll be set for life," we are in for a rude awakening when the industry we work in gets disrupted or our services are no longer needed.

Blind faith and true faith are two very different things. Blind faith is a way of saying, "Everything will work out," and then waiting for something to change. *True faith* requires that we put our faith in ourselves and our abilities, and use our knowledge about how money works to make sure we can move forward in a more positive direction.

If you are a freelancer, you know there are ups and downs in workload. Sometimes the job offers flood in, and sometimes you're sitting around waiting for an assignment. So naturally your income fluctuates too.

Seasoned freelancers are more aware of the unreliable nature of flow than most salaried workers, so they are better prepared for the ebbs in their business. They do not have a naïve expectation or blind belief that their income is guaranteed. Experience has showed them nothing is guaranteed.

Although they're less naïve than salaried workers, many are, instead, in constant worry mode. And that, we know, is not healthy either.

SEEKING THE OPTIMUM STATE: LAKE AND FLOW

The concept of *lake and flow* is simply the concept of abundance. When we're in a state of abundance, we feel as though we have enough in reserve to keep us safe and covered for a long time while maintaining a continual influx of money. Ah, what a great feeling!

If you've ever been in this situation, you know you don't have to worry about your day-to-day cash flow. Just like a large lake full of water that is fed by a stream of fresh-flowing water will be there for years to come, you can count on the fact that your money will be there too.

This is a situation I hope you will someday find yourself in. The key is to maintain enough stock and flow to provide not just for yourself but for others as well.

BUT DON'T GET STAGNANT: POND AND LITTLE FLOW

If you have enough stock but not much flow, your money becomes a pond with little flow as well. So you hang on to the money you have. The money doesn't come in as much, and there is not much flow going out. And what happens to a pond that isn't filtered? The water goes bad. There are plenty of examples in literature and history of this phenomenon. We need not look any further than Charles Dickens's Ebenezer Scrooge. A rich man with plenty of flow and assets holds on to his money, and his entire life deteriorates before him: he loses the love of his life, his only friend (Jacob Marley) dies, and he treats his employee terribly. The only way to clean a murky pond is to get the water out and move it through a filter. And if it's money you're hoarding in your metaphorical pond, you need to start spending it on others or charities you care about. There is simply no better filter for one's money.

THE JOY OF MONEY IS IN THE FLOW

I want you to imagine two types of people: One has a lot of money in the bank but doesn't want to spend it or participate in any activities; the other both earns and spends a lot of money on exciting events.

You can figure out easily whose life is more fun. It's in the experiences that we find the "fun" and joy in life. And flow is so much better with joy. It's one of the greatest "filtration" systems around.

STOCK IS SOLID BUT BORING

Even if you are lucky enough to have real estate or trust funds from your wealthy grandparents, if you are not doing anything in everyday life, you simply cannot be happy. No amount of money is going to make you happy. Happiness comes from experiences. Happiness comes from being, which implies being with others or doing things that enhance your life. Happiness comes from working—and, yes, earning money and participating in the flow. Most people who inherit a lot of money know this intrinsically. Without activity, there is boredom, and despair soon sets in. Having money, especially too much, can in some ways be just as stressful and life sucking as being poor. It may not seem that way to a poor person. You often hear people say things like "What does that rich person have to complain about? I wish I had his problems!" Well, no, you don't. Being perpetually bored, feeling useless, and having no purpose and direction is like being a prisoner who's serving a life sentence.

I know so many people dream of this situation. It's often idealized in a variety of ways. People think they don't want to have to work for money, but only because they have an unrealistic view of what being rich is like. The truth of the matter is that if you don't have a purpose or something to do every day, you'll end up becoming depressed.

I have met so many people with dead eyes who say they cannot feel joy and pleasure in everyday life. They go golfing and spend their evenings at parties. But after a while this type of life gets dull. There's no sense of fulfillment, no feeling of being a part of something bigger than one's own self. There is typically a higher rate of alcoholism and drug dependence among the extremely wealthy. Having a "pond" full of money is no guarantee of happiness.

Unless you find something that will give you joy and that will spread joy, you can never truly experience Happy Money.

IS CREATING A HEALTHY
STOCK AND FLOW POSSIBLE?

I am sure you have figured out by now that there is real security in having a healthy stock and flow. If you create enough stock and flow, then eventually you will feel no stress. The number will vary depending on your lifestyle, need, and priorities. So how do you figure out what realistically is a good amount for you?

If you set this number too high, you may find yourself in the same trap that so many other people are caught in: working continuously and never finding satisfaction.

For your own peace of mind, imagine how many assets and how much income are ideal for you. Then figure out who you know or admire who lives similarly. Study how they got to that place. If you have a personal relationship with that person, ask them for guidance. They may be eager to share their insights and knowledge. They themselves didn't get there by chance. After all, they, too, achieved their financial success with a certain mind-set.

If you work for a company and don't feel like you're advancing the way you wish, or feel that you could be doing more, then you need to step out of your comfort zone and ask for a job or a position that is more suitable for your talents. Find ways you can contribute more. As you move closer to where you can shine most, the power to attract people will increase, and so will your income.

One of the best and most common exercises to figure out your ideal financial situation is to imagine yourself five years from now. Take a moment and visualize this: Where do you see yourself financially? What do you want to see yourself doing? How do you think you can contribute your talents to the world? What does your lifestyle look like? Are you smiling? Happy?

Be bold here. I once coached a young housewife who imagined being a business owner. Within three years she was generating more income than her husband. Then imagine yourself in ten years. Ask yourself:

Now who am I?
What am I doing?
In what ways am I contributing?
What assets do I possess?
What is my income like?
How am I helping people?

If you take these steps, you will get there.

FAST AND EASY—WHEN MONEY DISAPPEARS FAST

I have coached many people about money. At the beginning, I always ask my clients how they make money. Some people make money by offering low-priced products and services. Others deal in high-priced ones, such as expensive jewelry. I can tell a lot about a person by the business ventures they choose to pursue. It seems obvious, but those who simply want to contribute in their own way and build a business little by little tend to choose modest businesses. And ambitious people tend to choose more expensive and riskier ventures—so they can make the biggest possible profit in one sale. They love to dress to impress and enjoy the finer things in life, like nice watches and designer handbags. They tend to drive more expensive cars too. In my experience, though, how people get their money—fast and easy or slow and steady—is also how they lose it.

For example, stories abound of once successful but now bankrupt business tycoons, celebrities, or people who inherited windfalls but lost it all in an incredibly short time. I have friends who have sold over a million copies of their books but lost their entire fortunes on one bad investment. I have another friend who lost all his money in the development of a new office space. The moral of the story is if you're not careful or mindful, the money you make will disappear quickly. Like people who win the lottery, if you don't feel like it is your money—that it is rightfully yours and that you earned it steadily, honestly, with great joy, and in the service of others—you tend to lose it.

The old adage applies here: "Fast money moves quickly away from you too."

SLOW MONEY WILL MAKE YOU RICH

Contrary to fast money, when money comes to you slowly, it is typically good for both business and life. People who become wealthy slowly and deliberately over time tend to keep the money for a long time as well.

One of the reasons I think people who earn money quickly lose it so fast is that they aren't prepared for it. They don't have a vast reservoir of experiences to draw on and they end up making hasty decisions, and usually those decisions are bad ones—primarily because the decisions are made largely out of fear. And as a rule, decisions made out of fear tend to be bad ones, based on the myth of scarcity rather than abundance.

One of the millionaire-producing occupations is, oddly enough, dry cleaning. Dry cleaners don't have the glamour and prestige of, say, jewelers, but their money is as good as anybody else's. Unlike jewelers, who have to work a sale over the course of several visits, a dry cleaner's business is steady. They charge very little but they do so every day. And if they can do it for a long time, they can become very wealthy. Repeatable income is where many fortunes are made.

So if you want to be rich, the first step you need to take is to find an occupation that you actually will enjoy and where you can thrive, grow, and contribute. Doctor, lawyer, accountant, dry cleaner, jeweler, business owner, chef, car detailer, writer, artist, singer . . . whatever you choose, it is absolutely possible to become a millionaire or successful. It's not *what you do*; it's *how you do it*. It may take time, but finding the place where your skills and talents shine is the most important thing you can do to guarantee your own success. It is perfectly okay to take ten years to figure out what to do. But once you find it and do it well, there will be nothing to stop you from being successful in no time. The first few years are slow for everyone, but once you establish yourself, you will start making Happy Money.

GO WHERE MONEY FLOWS

Money flows to where there is energy already. In other words, it will not go to a place where there is nobody or nothing.

So many opportunities are available in big cities like New York, London, Paris, Shanghai, and Tokyo.

Where many people gather, money goes.

That is why big cities tend to get bigger and attract more people from the suburbs and countryside. More than half the people in the world now live in big cities. And it is expected that more people will live in cities in the next few decades.

So if you want to make more money, city life is better than living in a forest. Granted, the Internet has changed some of that, but the reason why all the IT people gather in Silicon Valley is because there are many opportunities. With Internet business, it is easier to meet the investors, marketers, PR agents, and engineers.

Go where the people are.

People = energy = money.

When the flow of money is too big and too fast, you will have a hard time enjoying it. This can cause great "disturbances in the force." Imagine ten times more income and ten times more expenses and issues. If it happens too fast and you're not prepared, you could easily become overwhelmed. Some people don't even know what to do with that kind of flow. How do you know what the right amount of flow is for you? You'll know it by how it "feels." And that number will depend on the individual. Some people are okay with a $3,000 flow each month; some require much more. Some have so much, they can't even keep track of it and feel weighed down by their responsibilities.

Go for the flow that gives you the peaceful feeling!

Now that you understand how flow works, how to be a magnet for money, and what size flow you require to be at ease and happy in life, it's time to find the right flow to join.

Where do you find the right flow?

You'll know it when you join it. I know that sounds circuitous, because it is. Being in flow is being totally immersed in the moment. You feel no stress. Time seems to fly by. You're able to use your skills and talents effortlessly, and you're able to see how your work contributes and makes a difference. You know you're in flow because, oddly enough, it doesn't feel like working at all. Making Happy Money feels a lot like playing.

When you feel like you're playing, you've joined the right flow. If you haven't, you need to keep looking, keep searching.

Healthy people live in a fun flow of money. Because whatever they do, they tend to attract money, and they spend money in a way that makes them very happy.

They're the people who have no complaints about their lives.

If you become comfortable with the flow, you can share your flow with other people. One of the interesting things about money is that the more you let flow—i.e., the more that you share—the stronger flow grows.

Imagine two friends. One who always gives you tips, opportunities, and work, and refers clients to you. The other does none of those things. If you could give one of these two people a good deal, whom would you choose?

FINDING THE RIGHT TRIBE

In order to find the right flow, first you have to find your tribe. Your tribe is the group of people you resonate with. They appreciate what you do and who you are. They will support you and buy your products and services. They will keep you uplifted. And they are constantly rooting for your success and your rise. Your tribe doesn't necessarily have to be family. Given our global economy, they can be anywhere on the globe.

If you know which tribe you belong to, your life will become easier. It could be an artistic tribe, an academic tribe, or an entrepreneurial tribe. Whichever tribe you are in, once you belong there, you will feel a sense of homecoming, because the members of the tribe share many things. They appreciate how you feel, what you do, and, most importantly, who you are. When you're with your tribe, you feel safe and have a sense of belonging too. Whatever you do comes naturally.

FINDING MORE IN LESS

Constantly feeling that you deserve "more" is a dangerous way to live. It's simply impossible to keep getting more forever. But the pressure is there, everyone feels it, and everyone wants more. A greater number of children come home these days complaining of boredom, and parents feel more obligated to keep them entertained. Spouses feel pressure to make more money, go out more, and have more to offer each other. We feel guilty when we can't offer more. Everyone feels this desire for more, more, more to some extent, but we're not good at putting our feelings into words. Even our leaders and role models continually strive for more. Times are changing, though, and some of us are starting to get sick of this lifestyle.

As I mentioned earlier, when I was twenty-nine I entered a period of semiretirement to raise my daughter. I often joke that in the transition from more to less I found myself busier than ever. Ironically, I felt more stressed about my life at a time when I should have been taking it easy (or as easy as is possible for the stay-at-home dad of a growing toddler).

You can be insanely busy and still have peace of mind. Alternatively, you can have an empty schedule and be stomping on both your mental gas and brake pedals simultaneously. How long do you think you can go on like that before breaking down? In the age we are living in, our minds are more likely to spin at a thousand miles per hour during the moments when we have less to do.

Doing what you love and letting go of everything you don't need doesn't have to be a contradiction. All you have to do is stop and think about what you want and start moving in that direction. Imagine a life in which you interact only with people you love, in a place you love, doing only what you love. Do you think you'd be less happy, or be happy with less?

CREATING YOUR FLOW MEANS SHARING YOUR FLOW

You don't have to have something to start creating flow. Not all self-made millionaires had anything when they started.

Why did they become so successful later?

It is because they kept exchanging what they had for something better. First they started to share their heart or passion. People love to support someone who is passionate. Everywhere you go, passionate people are supported well. It is in our nature to want to support someone when we see they are working hard.

HOW MANY FRIENDS DO YOU HAVE?

I have no worries about money. It is not because I have a lot. It is because I have great friends. The other day I counted how many trustworthy friends I have. I could count more than fifty. So if I lost everything I have, I could go to a friend and ask them to let me stay for a week. I would be able to ask them to let me stay with their family. I could babysit, do the chores, listen to their life issues without judgment. I am a nice guest. I can clean the toilets, wash the dishes, and change lightbulbs. Then I could move on to another friend, and after fifty weeks I would be able to come back to the first friend and ask how they're doing. Even if I had no money, I could live for the rest of my life in peace and harmony.

Many people say that they don't have fifty friends or that this would be hard to do in a place like America, where you are expected to do everything on your own and by yourself; even children are expected to move out right after they finish school. This may be true now, but the culture is shifting and changing, and people all over the world are recognizing how important it is to have a strong network. So start small: Cultivate five or ten friends. Imagine asking each one if you could stay with them for a month until you got back on your feet. The goal of this story is not to point out how many friends you do or don't have to rely on; it's to emphasize that you need to start trusting life without money—as a mental exercise if nothing else. Chances are you will never need to live off your friends for a year, but there is enormous peace in knowing you wouldn't have to shoulder this burden entirely on your own. What you are afraid of is not the situation of losing or having no money. You are afraid of being alone. You are afraid of not being able to eat or live. But even if you have no money, if you can be certain you can count on friends or family who can support you graciously, then you have nothing to be afraid of. You'll feel only joy and appreciation, and that will manifest as a positive motivator in your daily actions.

Right now, so many people are trapped by their own fear. They can't leave a job they don't like because of fear. If they lose their job and income, they can't live, or so they tell themselves. But is that really, absolutely true?

The answer is no. There is always a way for you to live and thrive.

The first step is to see things from a different perspective.

True security does not lie in how much money you have. It lies in who you know and trust.

ALWAYS SAY *ARIGATO* TO THE MONEY!

My mentor Wahei Takeda once taught me the secret of money. The key to ensuring more of it, he said, is to thank the money when it comes in, and thank it again when it leaves you.

TRUSTING THE FLOW IS TRUSTING YOUR LIFE!

By now you know that trusting the flow of money is trusting in your future. You know that what you're worried about is not money. You are worried about your future. You worry whether you can keep the money you have or keep earning enough to survive. And that is a suffocating feeling.

Once you understand this psychological mechanism, you know you have to deal with your trust issues. Unless you clear those, it doesn't matter how much you have or how much you accumulate: you will never be able to stop worrying.

If you can trust life and the future, your money worries will disappear. You can count on yourself and you can count on your support network.

Trust your flow.

If you are experiencing a disturbance in the regular flow, this is a great opportunity to try something new. It may be time to create a different flow. If you feel stuck, call on someone you trust for help. Someone will show up to support you. If you don't ask for help, people will have no idea that you are in need of assistance. True, asking for help is hard to do, but it is fear that is keeping you from getting the help you need. You're afraid of what people will think of you, or you're worried people will judge you. Again, you have to replace that fear with trust. You have to believe that people are good and want to help you. And let me assure you, people love to help. There are more good people than you think. Once you feel free to ask for help, you will find that this world is full of happy and loving people who will come to support you.

I have learned how to ask for support over the years. At first you may feel embarrassed or a little awkward. But once you do this, it will get easier, and the results just may shock you. You never know what to expect. In a sense, it is total surrender. And when you surrender, miracles happen.

We've all heard stories of people asking or praying for help and then miraculously getting it. I assure you, once you've had such an experience, your world will never be the same.

HOW TO CREATE A HAPPY FLOW OF MONEY

There are several ways to create a happy flow if you don't have one already.

Here are my top ten ways to create a Happy Money flow:

1. Donate money.

Donating money to charity is a great way to feel the flow of Happy Money. You don't have to send a fortune; just a dollar can make a difference and make you feel good. Donating money to charity sends your brain and all the energy around you the message that you have more than enough. You have abundance, so you don't have to be afraid. Find a group or a charity that is meaningful to you and is in alignment with what you believe.

2. Give money to your friends.

You may have loaned your money in the past, and you may have been asked to give or invest money. The money given to your loved ones is always Happy Money. In life, everyone needs some money at a certain point. You may have enough resources. I have given money to people close to me who wanted to pursue their dreams, and you can feel when your money serves your friends and supports their lives. And there is no better feeling.

3. Send a gift to your friend.

Sending gifts to your friends is a fun way to spend money. In our house there is a closet for gifts. When we shop, we mostly shop for our friends.

The other day my wife and I went shopping. I am the one who pays and carries the shopping bags. On our way to the car I had both hands full of bags. Probably more than ten, including small ones. None of them were for us. They were all gifts. We couldn't find anything for us, but we found so many gifts for our close friends!

You don't have to buy expensive gifts. Just a small box of herbal tea is a great gift. Buying gifts for others makes them happy, and it makes *you* happy!

4. Give something extra—always.

If you give something—anything—always give something extra. When we are in a situation where we need to ask for help or to borrow something, we usually ask for less than what we really need because we feel shame in "not having." So when someone comes to you and asks for something, try to understand where their need is coming from and respond by giving more than they asked for. If someone asks to borrow a pen from you, give them a notebook too. If you are a boss hiring a new employee, give them a bit more than the salary they ask for. If you are negotiating a job with a client, see where you can throw in an extra service for free.

Giving extra in these situations transforms the reluctant, anxious energy into a positive force that leaves people feeling like they are cared for and loved. It is like making an investment in the emotional well-being of yourself and your community.

5. Pay more than you are asked.

This is the surprising one for a lot of people. When I get a bill, I pay as soon as possible. Sometimes I pay a little more than I was asked, to show my appreciation. This surprises a lot of people. They say they have never received more money than they asked for in their entire careers. When they get less than they ask for, they get upset. But when they get more, they are shocked.

I found it fun to pay more simply to see their reactions. People are not used to getting paid more. I feel it is my purpose to change people's minds about giving and receiving. It gives me great pleasure.

6. Send a gift or card to your clients or your boss.

We often forget how miraculous it is to keep getting money from clients or bosses. They could choose other people to give money to, but they found you and chose you. If you are a cleaner, for example, they could have gone to somebody else. But they came to you. Send your deepest appreciation with a card or a gift. Whenever I go to a bookstore and browse, I feel overwhelmed by the hundreds of bookshelves. Out of all the books, how could anyone pick *my* book? It seems almost impossible to find my book and buy it out of the hundreds of thousands of books available. I am deeply grateful for all my readers. To show your appreciation, send something to your clients. If you work in a company, your boss can be the one to thank.

What is interesting is that if you keep thanking them, they will remember your appreciation. When there is an opportunity, they are likely to give it to you because you are the first to come to mind.

7. Rejoice when you receive money.

When we receive money, most of us feel joy, but we are embarrassed to show it. Most of us have been taught to repress our feelings and to never, under any circumstances, talk about money. If you receive a birthday gift, it is okay to express joy, but for some reason we don't do this when we receive money. So please show your happy feeling whenever you receive money. If you show you are enjoying the money, people who gave it to you feel like doing it again to please you. It is fun to see a happy face. It is always great to feel and express your joy when you receive extra money.

The other day I got a two-dollar coupon at a grocery store. I said, "WOW, I am happy!"

The person next to me gave hers to me because she liked my smile. She wanted to see me smile for her two-dollar coupon. I gave her my best smile.

Have you ever done some shopping to make the shop owner you know happy? It could be a grocery store or diner. Giving a smile when people give you something is a powerful way to keep in flow.

8. Pray for happiness when you spend money.

This is something I learned from my mentor. Whenever I spend my money, I whisper in my mind, *May this money bless you and your loved ones*, because the money you spend will buy food or do something good for that person. Whenever you spend money, always bless the person or the company. By blessing them with your money, you are creating the Happy Money flow. Before you go to sleep, remember whom you gave money to that day, and imagine all the great things that will happen to them. If you live with that attitude, people notice who you are. Without your saying anything, people can feel the warm and loving energy that you carry.

9. Buy from someone you like.

With Internet shopping increasing, we do more shopping online. But it is really fun to buy from a real person. That is why there are still shopping malls and small vendors. If we continue to buy everything online, eventually there will be no physical stores, including the local mom-and-pop shops that are so integral to our happiness and way of life.

The reason there are still shops everywhere, I believe, is that people still want to see things, be inspired, and have human interaction. *We want to be where the people are, where there is great energy.*

When we have bought something from someone we like, even though we know we can get a better price somewhere else, we are keeping someone we like in business. We are keeping someone else happy and in their flow. So whenever you do go shopping, do so at your favorite place and buy from your favorite person. You will feel much better afterward.

You can do that online too. If you buy something from an Internet store you like, you will feel good because you spent Happy Money.

10. Be grateful for everything!

The most profound lesson in making and securing good fortune came to me from Wahei Takeda, my mentor. He once told me a story of a man who came to him in desperation. The man had massive amounts of debt and needed money. Wahei said he would give him the money but only if he said *arigato* (thank you) 100,000 times. That meant he would have to say *arigato* every minute of the day for months on end. The man agreed. By the time he went to borrow money, he no longer needed it. Why? His mindset of appreciation started to reap its own rewards. He was able to pay off his debts and no longer needed to borrow the money. When we say thank you, we release powerful energy into the world. We are instantly present. We realize everything we have is enough. *We* are enough. We have all that we need. Knowing this and feeling this is the most powerful force in the universe. You can literally achieve anything when you ground yourself in appreciation and gratitude.

Want to be wealthy? Happy? Peaceful? *Say thank you.* It's that simple.

CHAPTER 5

The Future of Money

In this chapter I want to explore the future of money. Not just the future of your own money, but the future of money's role in our world.

As our world changes, so, too, will our lives. The changes on the horizon are so amazing; they will no doubt defy the limits of our imaginations, but at the same time they have the potential to cause a lot of emotional chaos.

We also have to be realistic. The future holds some real challenges. In thirty years there will likely be 10 billion people on the planet, and the demand for food is projected to increase by 70 percent. The ocean is filling up with plastic trash. Climate change is affecting sea levels and agriculture. We have a large elderly population to take care of, various health crises to address, and increasing energy demands to meet. Meanwhile, class strife and political tensions abound.

Although we have our challenges, would you consider for a moment the world that we have inherited and the improvements we have made over the past two centuries? Many people live to be eighty years old or older. Infections that used to be life-threatening have largely been eradicated or contained. In most parts of the developed world, water isn't contaminated with cholera and parasites. The majority of countries live peacefully. We are not currently in the midst of a world war. And while war does exist and the potential for war is real in certain parts of the world, most countries rely on diplomacy to work out their differences. Advances in engineering and architecture have afforded us with homes and businesses that are climate-controlled. Many of us in the developed world rarely have to suffer from the harsh elements. We're also using power more wisely, and relying less and less on fossil fuels. And with all the advances in technology, we have more time than ever to spend entertaining ourselves and interacting with people outside our physical locations. Information that would have taken a considerable amount of time and energy to gather in the past now is literally at our fingertips in only seconds. We also have seemingly endless ways to pursue beauty, truth, meaning, and happiness.

Perhaps we live in a moment of too many revolutions. Perhaps there are just too many breakthroughs and game-changing discoveries for us to process all at once. Perhaps with all this change we are facing a different though no less profound crisis—an existential one. We know so much about our world and how it works—perhaps more so than at any other time in human history—but still there are gaps in our understanding. And because of these gaps, we can feel like we are just an accident of physics, or that our individual lives inhabit an insignificant timescale, or that we simply don't matter. Life, when defined as nothing more than an accident, can leave us feeling unmoored, without purpose, and devoid of hope. At its worst, life can be reduced to nothing more than aging, loss, suffering, and death, punctuated by only brief momentary pleasures. And within the confines of this definition, we can feel confusion and envy: *Why do some have so much and others so little? Why do some suffer endlessly and others seem to enjoy wealth, opportunity, fun, and joy?*

Despite all the advancements and improvements in our world, it is easy to stagnate, to feel despair, and to become overwhelmed by anxiety. So how can anyone transform their despair and anxiety? How can we transform the tendency to say, "What's the point?" How can we transform the voice in us that says, "You already made a mistake. Don't bother trying again. Just give up"?

This is the harmful, scarcity-based mind-set that I have warned you about. The problem with it is that it encourages us to betray what we could become in the future for the place where we are stuck at now. But we can transform our state of being when we decide to aim for something and commit ourselves to it. We can transform our lives when we decide to focus on gratitude and begin to act out of a sincere trust in life and the future.

It doesn't matter if you were born into a tough situation or if you put yourself there. You are part of an unfolding story, and the good news is this: you are the author of that story, and you get to determine the point of view. Your story can be a pursuit of happiness and a journey of adventure if you choose.

A REVOLUTION OF CONSCIOUSNESS

Thirty years ago, who could have imagined what the Internet would become? There hasn't been an information revolution like this since the printing press. People are starting to believe that the lecture halls of universities will soon be obsolete because lectures and audiobooks from the world's best professors and scientists can be shared with everyone.

Artificial intelligence (AI) is starting to have a big impact in the world, so take a minute to understand it better if you don't already.

AI, sometimes called machine intelligence, is basically a set of calculations that observes the world and learns how to maximize its success in achieving its goals. For example, if artificial intelligence is programmed into a bipedal robot trying to walk across a balance beam, the AI uses data gathered from previous failures as well as details about its surrounding environment to make self-correcting adjustments so that it can successfully cross the beam. The machine has the capacity to learn and adapt.

All kinds of things can be dramatically improved because of this. Artificial intelligence can do things like tell farmers which types of plants are best to plant. It is learning to identify early symptoms of diseases. It is creating new ways for companies to cut waste and improve supply chains.

There is much to be said about AI, and I am not an expert in the field. But it is important to have an understanding of what is possible, because we don't want our future actions to be based on fear of the unknown. The Institute for the Future (IFTF) estimates that 85 percent of the jobs that will exist in 2030 don't even exist yet. However, AI is not going to make every job obsolete; in fact, it will create the need for a variety of new jobs.

In addition to AI, there are all kinds of new industries that are exploring renewable energy and nontoxic materials. There are new strategies for removing plastic from the ocean on a massive scale. We are on the verge of being able to harvest and store enough solar and wind energy to power our homes and our cars. Even fusion energy is promising a future of abundant, clean energy.

This is important to keep in mind, because so many of us have an apocalyptic vision of the future. And that fear will certainly affect your mind-set negatively.

In this chapter I want you to stretch your own imagination regarding what is possible—what may be possible. How can we change ourselves and our mind-sets and our goals so that we can realize a future of maximum prosperity and happiness? AI is here, and it is already changing the way we live, and I believe it has the power to change our consciousnesses too. When we start to push the boundaries of what is possible in the physical realm, we can push the boundaries in the energetic realm as well. And we will ultimately push the boundaries of the way we think about the energetic quality of money and the role it will play in our lives.

FUTURE MONEY

Our lives are the result of all the mistakes and achievements of human history. Ever since our species realized that we could turn a tree branch into a tool, our species has been carving that metaphorical tree branch into a spear, and today we have a very, very fine-pointed spear.

But how do we use it for the ultimate good?

Well, you first have to aim at something. What you aim at determines how the world unfolds before you. There is a lot of liberation in that truth. Think about it: if you decide to turn your gaze toward something, your reality becomes what you are looking at. Therefore, aim at the best thing that you can think of!

It isn't only a matter of our natural abilities or what tools we hold, because the all-important variable is what we decide to aim at.

I think that a happy future for money will be one where the number of privileges in society that do not cost money or are very affordable will greatly increase. Things that we deem essential for well-being will become abundant, accessible, and inexpensive if not free. Education, communication, energy, quality food, and all kinds of opportunities won't be primarily based on the accumulation of money. This is already being demonstrated in the sharing economy. People are learning how to put things to greater use and how to share the gains.

Money has not always been inextricably tied to our survival, and I don't think it always will be. There is no doubt that money is useful, and we will always need a way of exchanging energy among ourselves. But money will gradually cease to feel like an energy that controls our destinies.

I think that money can become something more like salt. There is a fantastic book called *Turning Oil into Salt: Energy Independence Through Fuel Choice* by Gal Luft and Anne Korin, which is about creating alternative energy sources. The book draws on the history of salt, because for a long time salt was the only way to preserve food so that you could survive through the winter. This meant that salt was an all-important resource. Societies knew exactly where their salt came from, how much they had in reserve, and its value in relation to other things. It was, in other words, their currency. But when canning, refrigeration, and other food preservation methods came about, salt suddenly became much less crucial. Salt is obviously still something that is needed and used today, but our survival through winter does not hinge on salt. And now salt is abundant and inexpensive.

Oil is now like what salt used to be. Oil has a lot of value right now because we have no other option for powering our cars, planes, and ships. The control of oil is a cause of friction between nations, just like money is a cause of friction between people. But slowly we are finding alternatives to the gasoline-fueled engine. And eventually oil will go the way of salt. We will still use it for some things, but it will be abundant and inexpensive. I think money will eventually go the way that oil is destined to go.

The point is not that we will live in a world free of money; we will live in *a world free of fear of lack of money*. That is the key difference. We're finally getting to a point in our collective consciousness when we are no longer linking money with freedom. We no longer need money to feel happy, safe, and free. We know this because we know that happiness, security, and personal autonomy is an inside job. And all it requires is that we be present, that we be engaged in the moment, and that we use our time and talents to do what we love.

TWO VERY DIFFERENT OUTLOOKS
TOWARD MONEY IN THE FUTURE

Where you are in your consciousness and development will affect your outlook on the future of money: it may be a very pessimistic outlook or a very bright one. This is how I see the two:

The optimistic, abundant mind-set sees all the jobs of the future: research, engineering, art and design, entertainment, food and nutrition, health care, space technology, waste management, renewable energies, and all the things that have to do with AI. Not only will all of these jobs continue to be needed, but their fields will expand with new leaps in technology. And even as more jobs are replaced with autonomous machines, many things will still require a human touch and people will continue to value human design and craftsmanship. Education will become more and more accessible in the sense that anyone can get resources for higher-level education on the Internet. It is just a matter of organizing new systems.

And while it is true that drivers, factory workers, field laborers, accountants, and other forms of middle management in white-collar industries will be reduced to algorithms, sensors, and robots, in the optimistic vision of the future, our response to these changes will be one of excitement, gratitude, love, and a sense of adventure.

The pessimistic or scarcity mind-set, on the other hand, sees a future of class struggle in which the wealthy feel the need to hoard their money and invest only in things that serve their own narrow interests, while the middle and working classes feel resentment. And of course this ill will becomes a barrier to their own creativity, productivity, upward mobility, and happiness.

This mind-set says, "We're doomed." It blames AI and technology for all of the world's problems. It is totally fear based and argues that AI is going to make a huge percentage of the jobs we take for granted today obsolete. This mind-set believes that an AI-centric world will result in a cold and unfriendly society where corporate interests' desire to make a buck outweigh the individual's basic rights and needs. You don't have to imagine this type of future mind-set. So many people today already believe this myth of division and unfairness. So many already feel slighted and forgotten. Fear dominates our news headlines and most of the political rhetoric around the globe, only deepening the divide between rich and poor. The rich constantly feel like their money is taken away to help others, and the poor feel like they are taken advantage of by the rich. No one is happy and everyone is afraid.

But it doesn't have to be this way.

YOU CAN CHOOSE YOUR FUTURE

I think that we will likely end up somewhere in the middle—somewhere between the optimistic and pessimistic outlooks on the future. There is a constant tension between these two mind-sets, and that is why we have the mixed outcome in the world that we see today. But just as we looked at the total of positive and negative outcomes in civilization, we can clearly see that our well-being has been improving on the whole, and even exponentially as time goes on. And all the things that have happened have been a result of the decisions made by people just like you.

We really do have the power to choose how we will enter into the future.

In terms of your personal money, you have the power to choose how you relate to it. You can have a lot or a little. You can have a happy flow or an unhappy flow. You can make the people around you happy with your money or use money to make people feel miserable. You can choose to take a risk, to set your aim toward your favorite things, or you can choose to try to avoid risk, to stay safe, to cling to what you have and what you know. But whichever outlook you choose, you will find it reflected back to you.

Therefore it's up to you. And your choices will affect not only your future but the future of your family and that of the people around you as well. If you are happy with money and life, you can expand the conditions for happiness to those around you. In order for you to expand, you have to begin within the limits of your own being—that is, to have a good relationship with your money and to create the flow of Happy Money in the areas that you are responsible for.

If you can do that, the ripple effect of Happy Money will touch many people around you. Once people see how fun it is to live in the flow of Happy Money, they will try to create their own best version of Happy Money too.

You can start the wave that ripples into everyone's lives right now. It is easy to start.

Just say thank you when the money comes in, and say thank you again when it goes out.

You will feel different in everyday life once you start this flow by yourself. When others do the same with you, you will feel connected with them.

WHAT IS IMPORTANT TO YOU?

When asked this question, most of us will say "family" and "friends." Those are good answers. But let me ask the question again, a little differently this time. What would someone watching you say is important to you based on the way you act in your daily life? We all talk about some lofty values, but our real values show themselves in the way we act every day. Where and how you spend your time and energy is what is important to you.

So now I ask you again: What is important to you?

Maybe it is time to reconsider what is really important to you. This is a great first step for joining the flow of Happy Money. People who are clear about their values know what they are thankful for, and that in turn serves as a guiding force through all of what life can throw at you.

You might have heard advice like "Always work hard with a smile, even if it is for a low wage and you don't love it, because you never know who is watching." People get recognized for their talent and passion all the time. Yet I think this is the sort of message that a lot of people become tired of hearing, because so many people never get that lucky chance even though they feel like they are working so hard. And I'll let you in on a little secret: *It isn't chance that gets you closer to the things you want.*

Rather, it's intentional gratitude. The people who express gratitude often and consistently for what they have are the people who end up taking responsibility for their own happiness. They have a heart that is always saying thank you. And so, when it comes time to act, they are responsible— or, as I like to think of it, *response-able.* They have the ability to respond. They can navigate through the times of suffering, and they can also really enjoy the good times. They are able to be honest with themselves and others because they aren't hiding from anything. They do their jobs with sincerity because they are actually sincere. A person like that is destined to create opportunities in their life. It is just a matter of time and the way it happens. It's not up to chance. It's not up to someone else. It's simply one's own *response-ability* to be grateful for what they have and be able to seize opportunities as they arise. When you are mired in self-pity or you believe you have no responsibility for your own success—that it is up to chance or someone "discovering" you—then you are destined to be unhappy. Without gratitude, happiness is all but impossible.

The emotional state of the future depends on a willingness to inherit the abundance available to us and a willingness to take responsibility for the challenges. If we do this, our world will become charged with positive energy, and so will our money.

HAPPY MONEY WILL CHANGE YOUR FAMILY

It's one thing to be at peace with yourself about money, which in itself isn't always such an easy thing to do. But as we have been discussing, expressing gratitude and being in the present moment create the conditions for Happy Money.

Still, life isn't lived solo. You have a family or a partner, and they have emotions toward money too. They are playing their own money game, and as most of us know, our different ideas about money can and do collide, usually with distressing consequences.

What I have learned over years of counseling families about money is that honesty is the absolute priority for creating a system of Happy Money within a family.

Parents usually hide their financial situation from their kids, and just tell them something like "When you are older, you will understand how hard life is." The problem with this is that it prolongs the immaturity of their children. If you treat children as if they are naïve, they will continue to be naïve children and will always be asking why they can't do this or have that. Everything will be "unfair" to them. But if you treat your children like adults, they will respond to that. If you tell them more about money—what it takes for you to make it, what kinds of bills you have, how you are planning to spend or save—they will gradually start to relate to you. They will start to act like little adults who are responsible for their family's situation. The families I have seen that are the happiest are very transparent about money, and other things too, with their children.

The same goes for the relationship between couples. Even though the members of a couple are both adults, sometimes one partner will treat the other like a child who doesn't need to know or doesn't have the capacity to understand their financial situation. Or maybe they aren't transparent because they fear having a fight. Maybe they are trying to cover up their mistakes. This is why honesty is just so incredibly important.

THE FLOW OF HAPPY MONEY
CAN CROSS GENERATIONS

We are so used to the myths of scarcity and the winner-take-all mentality that when we experience a true act of generosity, it can really stick with us. It is so special that it has the power to change a life. Even the word *arigato* in Japanese literally means "difficult to be," so when we say *arigato* to someone, we are complimenting them for making such a difficult and special gesture.

Once I heard a story about a man whose grandfather was a very successful businessman. He was generous, and the people whom he touched respected and loved him. But as is often the case, his grandson was spoiled and didn't have a sense for business, and he went bankrupt and lost all the money and the estate that his grandfather had built.

The grandson and his family were forced to move into a small apartment. One day he was visited by a stranger who looked very old. The stranger explained to the grandson that when he was a boy, he had been an orphan, but because of the generosity of the man's grandfather, he was given a job. He also recalled being given sukiyaki, a traditional Japanese dinner served in a hot pot, at the grandfather's home. It always made the stranger smile to think of the warm and delicious meals—not to mention the friendship and generosity shown to him by the man's grandfather. "Your grandfather was always so kind to me; he taught me everything about business and life. Consequently, I owe all the success I have enjoyed in life to your wonderful grandfather." The grandson was taken aback. "So what business do you have with me?" he asked. The stranger explained, "I heard about your financial situation and I searched for you. I'd like to give you this as a gesture of my appreciation for all the kindnesses your grandfather showed me." The stranger then proceeded to hand him a big package, which included a sukiyaki set for his family. Later, after they had pulled the large pot out of the box to make dinner, his children found an envelope at the bottom of the box. In the envelope was a check large enough to cover the cost of a house. Attached to the check was a brief memo: "Please use this money to restore life to your family."

The once ungrateful and spoiled grandson was so moved and influenced by this gesture—what we can now call Happy Money—that he, too, was transformed. He spent the stranger's money wisely and became very successful. Even fifty years after the fact, the energy of Happy Money had the power to change lives in a positive way.

FIND ABUNDANCE IN YOURSELF AND SECURITY IN PEOPLE, NOT MONEY

We tend to think that if we have a lot of money, our lives will be secure. This is why everyone—rich and poor alike—wants more money. Everyone wants to be safe, to know that everything is taken care of. And this is exactly why we also have so much fear when it comes to money.

But money doesn't always bring security. So what does?

Relationships. There is nothing more secure than the deep and profound bond of a lasting relationship. And if everyone could rely on everyone else to have their back during difficult times, then there would be no need for "fear" to be related to money. If you are seriously seeking security, then go to your friends and family. And, yes, that also means that instead of worrying endlessly about saving and investing, you invest your time in relationships. You will not only feel better, but also can rest assured that you will have support when the time comes.

Stop attaching your sense of security to money, and soon you'll discover the freedom that comes with not worrying incessantly about money.

PLAN YOUR WAY OUT OF THE "MONEY GAME"

We are all stuck with money at some level. But we can start to free ourselves if we view how we interact with money as a game. The game is very different for the wealthy and the financially challenged. But whichever game you find yourself playing, there is one thing they have in common: a game is something played against others.

How do we know if we are playing the game well? Well, we look around at the competition. We check to see how others are doing compared with ourselves. We frame the situation as though we are scoring points, or others are scoring on us, and we use this arbitrary system to judge how well we are doing.

Do we ever feel like we are winning this game? Maybe at times we do. But just when you think you're winning, you see someone else's life and suddenly begin to think, *I've got to have a life like them!* We send a message to our brains that says, *I am not enough.*

That is why no matter how much we earn and save, we still feel like we are losing the game. Most of us feel miserable even if we are doing well.

The psychological effect of this game makes every player feel like a loser. Super-wealthy people feel bad because the big summer house and the private jet are no replacement for solid relationships and true meaning in life. The middle class feels bad because they are wearing themselves out trying to prove their worthiness to others. Low-income people become dejected and give up on the idea that they can achieve their dreams.

How do we get out of this vicious cycle? I suggest that you forget about the "opponents" and start playing the game with yourself. *Instead of comparing yourself with others, compare who you are today with who you were yesterday.* After all, the only one really judging you is you. It may feel as though other people are judging you, and maybe they are, but I have found that this is not the case as often as we think. You might be surprised at how many people are actually jealous of something about you.

I have many opportunities to meet very wealthy people, and one question I always like to ask them is: "When did you feel like you were wealthy?" I expected they would respond: "When I earned my first million dollars [or $5 million or $10 million or maybe even $100 million]." But their answer is always the same: "I don't think I am wealthy." They may follow that with something like: "My friend has a private jet, but I can't afford one." Even if the "wealthy" person owns a major company, more houses than family members to live in them, and more money than they would need to survive several lifetimes, they still don't feel wealthy. Since you can't control who has more than you do, it makes sense to find another way to determine when you finally have enough or when you can call yourself wealthy. And the best way to do that is to play the money game with yourself.

The money game as it is currently set up is designed to make you compare yourself with others and therefore want more and more, even though you don't need it. Since this is a global phenomenon, it is hard to escape. If you try to get out of that game, there is pressure to come back in to live like everybody else does. Once you leave the game, you will feel very different. You may work at the same place and make the same amount of money, but you will be happier because you no longer need to live up to other people's expectations. You willfully decide on a new set of rules of engagement for the game. It's no longer about acquiring more property, or having more stuff, or doing more than your "opponents."

Instead you choose what makes you feel like a winner: a job you love (it can be the job you already have) or switching careers to better match your abilities and talents. Or perhaps money isn't your only yardstick for "winning"—perhaps instead it is more time to spend with friends and family, or more flexibility to pursue hobbies and interests, or to do whatever it is that brings you happiness and joy. You may even see this time as an opportunity to discover talents and gifts hidden within you. Ask yourself: *What excites me? What do I do really well?* I know that if you do something you're excited about and you do it well, you will eventually attract all the money and clients you'll ever need.

But that's not to say it's going to be easy or that you don't need to learn the basics about money: earning enough, saving just enough, and spending enough too. If you do this, I can assure you, as I have seen it myself countless times, that you'll be financially free in a three- to seven-year time frame. Anyone can do it if he or she is committed to doing it. Many also find great joy supporting others in doing the same. By helping other people, they gain a deep sense of connection and happiness.

This is a ripple effect of happiness. You don't have to become a millionaire to start the flow of Happy Money. Imagine the kind of world we could create if the majority of people decided to free themselves from the money game! Think of the possibilities!

Here's what I think could happen if we *all* start tapping into and contributing to the flow of Happy Money:

Wealthy people will share bigger portions of what they have with less fortunate people. Middle-class people will take more risks and start doing what they love. People with financial difficulties will feel more secure and find more hope for the future and benefit from the support of the wealthier classes. As a result, there will be less fighting in families, less crime, and—dare I say it?—more peace in society too.

If we free ourselves from fear-based and negative thought cycles and instead become more present and do more of what makes us feel happy, we will undoubtedly create an atmosphere in which we can all support and encourage one another.

YOU CAN START OVER EVERY DAY

When you are totally connected to the present and living by your own rules, you can start over anytime you want. You don't have to let the troubles or failures of the past paralyze you in the present.

You create your own terms. If not, you'll be constantly controlled by "conventional wisdom"—those money myths that tell you that you aren't enough.

You don't have to make, save, and spend money like other people do. You don't have to feel embarrassed about not getting new things or buying the latest model of everything. You can wear the same T-shirt or fleece every day and feel perfectly fine. You don't need material things to judge how good you are; you know that you are good! You decide how much you actually need to make and save, and you don't spend your energy on things that don't contribute to your own idea of success.

If you can find happiness in your own unique lifestyle, that is the sign that you're moving out of the money game. There are no right answers. You can find your state of happiness in simplicity and minimalism. Or if making a lot of money and creating a big flow is your preference, go for it. Only you can say what is right for you.

So create your rules and stick with them. Don't let other people decide for you what to wear, where to live, how much you need to have in the bank to retire, where to vacation, where to work, or what to do. By reclaiming the choices in your life, you reclaim your freedom regardless of your bank statement, and that is truly where the Happy Money is. Most of all, do it with the idea of Happy Money in mind, and become a shining example of what it means to be both happy and wealthy.

DEFINE YOUR OWN HAPPINESS

A few years ago I had the privilege of going to Bhutan to do research for my book about happiness. The country of Bhutan is called one of the happiest nations in the world. Before I went there, I imagined everybody went around smiling and saying hello with an open heart to strangers. But when I was there, I saw that you are lucky if anyone smiles at you. Many of the people are shy, so they hide when they spot a foreigner. They have a very modest and simple lifestyle. I realized that they don't have an attitude like "Look at me! I am so super-happy!" It is more a quiet happiness. They are content with their everyday life and simply satisfied with what they have.

I asked them what they worried about, and I was surprised when many of them said they had no worries at the moment. They have a free health care system, and if something happens, they believe their friends or the king will help them. If I asked the same question in an industrialized country, I would probably have to spare a good half hour to listen to their complaints about their work, partners, kids, and government.

In Bhutan, however, almost every person I interviewed was satisfied with their life. They weren't caught up in a game of comparing or judging one another. One of them said, "I have a great family. I have a job and a house. Is there anything else that I need?"

I was shocked. He was right. What else does he really need to feel happy?

But we live in a totally different world from Bhutan. They have a simple, minimal life, and that is what works for them.

This is exactly what we can learn from them. Not that we have to revert to some primitive sort of living, but whether or not we are actually aware of what works for us. Happiness is something that we define for ourselves. Because if we get caught up in the money game of comparisons, then we feel pushed to think that happiness means MORE. That's what got us to the "Work harder, work more, and you'll achieve your dreams" myth we all so readily bought into over the past century. But, really, what have we gotten? More stuff? More stress?

After I returned home from Bhutan, I took an inventory of my own life. *We have so much more than they have*, I thought. *But are we happier?* And the reality was no. The people of Bhutan were doing a better job of being happy.

We don't have to live like those in Bhutan to be happy. But, like the Bhutanese, we have to decide for ourselves what is enough for our happiness.

DO WHAT MATTERS MOST AND LET MONEY SUPPORT YOU!

As I approach the end of this book, I want to say this to you:

> *You have the freedom to choose your life.*
> *You can do whatever you want.*
> *Don't let money stop you.*

We are afraid of so many things. We think it is about money, work, and people, but it is really about us and our fear of the future. We should not be fooled by anxiety and fear. Whatever we fear usually doesn't become reality, and yet we waste so much of our energy on worrying. It's such a waste of our time, talents, and potential.

Take a risk when you feel like you are being called to do so. It is usually the right direction and lifts you to the next level.

How do you know what risk to take? It will be the choice to do what matters most to you.

Don't let your fear stop you.

We are born with great gifts. The gifts you have are ready to come out.

Unfortunately, most of us don't discover our gifts. The true tragedy of our lives is that we don't even know what gifts we possess. I didn't know that I could write until I started at the age of thirty-four. I was one of those folks who was surprised by what they could do! And I am sure you have some gifts inside of you waiting to surprise you too!

So many gifts go unnoticed and forgotten because of fear—fear of trying, fear of failure, fear of not measuring up to someone else's ideas of who or what we should be, and fear of not having enough money to survive.

Unless you believe in yourself and your gifts, no one else will. Your parents, your friends, and your partner may wish you happiness, but they can't bring out your great gifts in the way that you can. Because gifts show their shape and power only when you use them.

After I became a successful author, I attended a high school reunion at my former all-boy Jesuit school. At the reunion most of my friends and teachers were surprised to learn that I had become an author. They had all thought I would end up being an accountant like my father. Writing was the last career they had thought I would pursue. But I am actually the one who is most surprised. Most of us are shocked to find what true gifts are buried deep within us.

I have found that your gifts show up when you are ready to take responsibility for your own life. For some reason they announce themselves to us when we realize that we have only ourselves to count on for our happiness. That realization switches on all your senses and makes you feel ALIVE.

But it's not enough to just discover the gift. You have to put that gift into action. You have to get serious about improving your gifts. If you want your gifts to create value for others and to make money, then you have to put the time in to excel—and ultimately sell your services.

Eighteen years ago, I had a dream about my daughter that woke me up to the importance of using my gifts. In the dream, my young daughter appeared to me, asking me why I wasn't doing anything to change the world. I made excuses like "Look, I am nobody. I am not a politician or professor and I don't know about all these complicated world issues. I can't change the world!" And in the dream I saw her eyes narrow in disappointment. That was the last thing I saw before I woke up. It was such a bitter dream that it shook me to my core. I felt so small and ashamed. I didn't want to let my daughter down. And so I didn't. I thought about my life and my unique experiences that had shaped my skills and abilities. I didn't have to wait for inspiration or go looking all around for it. My gifts shouted out to me, "*Here I am!*"

A few years later I started to write books on happiness and money in the hope that our world would become a better place. At that time I had no idea how it was going to go or what impact my work would ultimately have. But, to my amazement, the audience for my work has continued to grow, and I know my messages are in fact impacting millions of people's lives.

And now I am passing the baton.

You are next in line to start something that will make a difference in this world—something that excites you so much that you can't help but do it; something that fills your life with meaning; something that contributes to the people around you.

FIVE STEPS TO HAPPY MONEY

I am going to wrap up this book by giving a quick summary, a quick list of five steps you can take, starting today, that will get you into the flow of Happy Money:

I. Shift out of the scarcity mind-set.

Each person has the ability to choose what kind of money mind-set they want to live with. That is why the first step to Happy Money is to get yourself into an abundant mind-set. Until now we have been taught to believe that money is scarce and that we have to get it before someone else does. We have become a culture that is obsessed with money. We are so focused on the amount of money that we do or don't have that it cuts off our potential for a great life.

Why? Because we automatically assume that we won't be able to make a living if we take a risk and go for what we really want. The concept that there is not enough in the world makes us feel small and less generous. Don't let your mind-set limit your life's potential. If you have an abundant mind-set, you start seeing new possibilities, you become more creative, and you become more capable of responding to difficulties in life. You free yourself to create your own destiny.

2. Forgive and heal your money wounds.

We know that our attitudes about money are mostly inherited. And the people whom we inherited those ideas from also inherited theirs. But you won't get to Happy Money if you let this become cause for resentment. The people who went before you were young, inexperienced, and prone to all sorts of mistakes. You know this because you have been there too. Imagine the situation that your parents were in. They acted out of fear because they didn't know any other way. They did what they had to do. If you can sympathize with their situation and their humanity, you can begin to understand why they made the mistakes they did. Then you can forgive them, and when you do, your heart will feel lighter. You can break the cycle of Unhappy Money by forgiving others and, just as importantly, by forgiving yourself for the mistakes you've made.

You can set the tone for a new era of Happy Money when you forgive and begin the process of healing. When we make peace with the past, those wounds cease to be an obstacle to our present happiness, and money stops feeling like a mysterious, uncontrollable force. That is what gives us the freedom to find the Happy Money flow that works for us.

3. Discover your gifts and get into the flow of Happy Money.

Everyone is born with certain gifts. Some people find them when they are young; others may need time to search. Uncovering your talents, and finding what brings you joy, is one of the most important things in life. If you are no longer burdened by the past, you will be surprised at how quickly your talents will be revealed to you. When you take an inventory of your life, all the dots begin to connect. Getting into a state of flow will become second nature. Difficulty and struggles will transform into fun and adventure right before your eyes. When you start sharing your gifts with the world, you kick-start the flow of Happy Money. Knowing who you are and where you feel most alive is what creates the groundwork for trust, because you have nothing to hide from.

The more you develop your gifts and the more you share your gifts, the more Happy Money you will attract. People who are successful in all kinds of fields credit their success to a love for what they do.

4. Trust life.

Trust is a major part of a happy state of being. Once you can truly trust in yourself and in those around you, life gets so much easier. Those everyday anxieties about the future begin to fade away. When everyone is looking out for each other with hearts and minds of abundance, we all become free to share and receive all the great things that money can do. There is no fear of what might happen in the future, because we know that we can count on people, and they can count on us.

Trust and fear cannot coexist. It is one or the other. Trust makes us more active, creative, and free, whereas fear stifles our actions, counters our intentions, and creates resentment. When we trust, we are free from expectations. Risk no longer feels like risk. Almost all the things that we worried would turn out terribly actually turn out to be some of the most positive things in our lives. The "bad" things that have happened to us end up working in our favor.

We know that everything that happens, positive or negative, will end up working out to support our lives in its own unique way. This is what frees us from the paralyzing anxiety of judging things in our lives as "good" and "bad." That is why trusting people are more passionate and successful.

When we trust, we are able to become our authentic selves.

5. Say *arigato* all the time.

A world of Happy Money looks like a world in which everyone is continually expressing a deep appreciation for the energy that flows through their lives. A willingness to give and receive, rather than keep a tight clutch on what we have, is what creates the conditions for Happy Money. The positive energy of gratitude works *for* us and invites more money into our lives.

There are two kinds of people: those who are outwardly appreciative and those who always find something to blame or complain about. Which do you think is a more magnetic personality?

People who appreciate life are more liked, more approachable, and more attractive. As a result, they invite all kinds of opportunities into their lives.

We know that there will be times when things don't go exactly as we planned. But a heart that says *arigato* in the face of it all gives us an inner resolve that navigates us right through all kinds of rough waters.

So take every chance you get to show your gratitude. Show appreciation for yourself. If you live in the flow of gratitude, your life will be full of unexpected miracles. When we are in this kind of flow with our inner self, and with those around us, we live with Happy Money!

YOUR LIFE IS MADE UP OF EXPERIENCES

When you are about to die, you won't be worrying about how much money you made or how much you have in the bank. I highly doubt that on your deathbed you will be checking your bank balance. You will remember all the people you loved and the things you did. With any luck, you'll be surrounded by those who loved you most when the time comes for you to depart this earth.

The moral of the story: What you own isn't the most important thing in life. People are. *You* are. So focus on your life, what makes you feel most alive while you're here, and create as many wonderful memories as you can. Spend your time, your money, your energy—your Happy Money tokens—on the people who matter most to you, the people you love and appreciate. Be mindful of what you spend your money on: *Is it where your love is? Is it where your truest, best, happiest self is?*

Chances are you may not need a lot of money to make memories with your loved ones. Be creative. Whatever you are going to do, be open to many possibilities. Opportunities open up when you are creative—when you take risks, feel appreciative, hopeful, and abundant, and are open to receiving.

My hope is that if you treat yourself and your loved ones with gratitude, kindness, and love, life will treat you in kind. I pray for your peace, happiness, and prosperity.

This book is my prayer for you. May all the blessings and Happy Money come to you!

And, finally, *arigato*!

Thank you.

Acknowledgments

Writing this book has been more rewarding than I could have ever imagined.

I am so thankful to everyone who has provided inspiration, guidance, and support in the writing of my first English book, especially my agents, Celeste Fine and John Maas, my editor Jeremie Ruby-Strauss, and the entire Simon & Schuster team. And a special thank-you to my editor Mary Curran Hackett and the entire Kevin Anderson & Associates team. I'd also like to thank Brian Weiland and Sarah Vanderwater for helping with my English writing.

Special thanks for their friendship, mentorship, and support: Gary Zukav and Linda Francis, Jack and Inga Canfield, John and Bonnie Gray, Ivan and Beth Misner, Tony Robbins, Brian Tracy, Robert Kiyosaki, Jim Rogers, Allan and Barbara Pease, Janet B. Attwood, Chris Attwood, Alan Cohen, DC Cordova, Dave Asprey, Lynne Twist, Marci Shimoff, Patty Aubrey, Joe Vitale, Debra Poneman, Kute Blackson, Barnet and Sandi Bain, Lisa Garr, JJ Virgin, Junki Yoshida, Robert Allen, Eric Pearl, Darryl Anka, Patrick Newell, Scott Mills, James Hummel, Douglas Fraser, Lynn

Robinson, Rocky Liang, Hafsat Abiola, John Wood, Pam
Grout, Barnett Cordero, Robert Shinfield, John Demartini,
Roice Krueger, Raymond Aaron, Arjuna Ardagh, Blaine
Bartlett, Daniel and Sandra Biskind, Pete Bissonette, Ray
Blanchard, Nicole Brandon, Rinaldo Brutoco, David Buck,
Susan Budinger, Peggy Cappy, Sonia Choquette, Dawson
Church, Cheryl Clark, Scott Coady, Steve D'Annunzio,
Verónica de Andrés and Florencia Andrés, Zen Cryar
DeBrücke, Scott deMoulin, Bobbi DePorter, Marie Dia-
mond, Mike Dooley, Ken Druck, Eric Edmeades, Joan
and Stewart Emery, Roxanne Emmerich, Cindy Ertman,
Cheryl Esposito, Steve and Veronica Farber, Arielle Ford,
Amy Fox, Vivian Glyck, Deirdre Hade, Roger Hamilton,
Phyllis Haynes, Alexandria Hilton, Sam Horn, Raz Ingrasci,
Lisa Janelle, Fred Johnson, Sandra Joseph, Cynthia Kersey,
Jim Kwik, Vishen Lakhiani, Natalie Ledwell, Shelly Lefkoe,
Chunyi Lin, Fabrizio Mancini, Adam Markel, Howard
Martin, Jennifer McLean, Lynne McTaggart, Dave Meltzer,
Monica Moran, Dianne Morrison, Mary Morrissey, Dr. Sue
Morter, Lisa Nichols, Gabriel Nossovitch, Yasmin Nguyen,
Guillermo Paz, Dawa Tarchin Phillips, Carter Phipps, Srini
Pillay, Marc Pletzer, Andrés Portillo, Mike Rayburn, James
Redmond, Robert Richman, Sonia Ricotti, Matt Reimann,
Joel and Heidi Roberts, Martin Rutte, Sheri Salata, Anita
Sanchez, Sadhvi Saraswati, Paul Scheele, Yanik Silver, Mari
Smith, Colin and Gabi Sprake, Bettie Spruill, Donna Stein-
horn, Guy Stickney, Carl Studna, Terry Tillman, Phil Town,
David Wagner, GP Walsh, Matt Weinstein and Geneen

Roth, Christy Whitman, Marcia Wieder, David Wood, Sandra Yancey, Tyson Young, Chichi, Vicky, Sean Gallagher, and Miki Agrawal.

Also, I'd like to thank my Japanese mentors and friends: Sakurai, Otha, Minami, Satoh, Ueki, Oshigane, Okamura, Ureshino, Iinuma, Moriue, Nagasawa, Ohsato, Shimizu, Yokota, Nakamura, Yoshio, Satoh, Nishida, Motonishi, Nishizono, Raimu, Kanemoto, Toshi and Chieko, Jaian, Midori, Torii, Shige, Itoh, Suzuki, Toyo, Sachin, Taku, Anaguchi, Hara, Chris, Ken, Tei, Takuma, Natsumi, Yohei, Madoka, Hamio, Hiro, Haya, Tetsu, Ohiro, Hina, Yoshi, Shinichi, Kenichi, Akifu, Shige, Taku & Yumi, Kochi, Tamami, Yasumiko, Rich, Akina, Kuro, Masaya, Sara, Nori, Tomo, Suekichi, Shin, Monica, Saori, Mari, Miwa, Kuni, Hyoga, Takano, Ryo, Hide, Izurin, Kurumi, Kei, Jonny, Yoko, Toshi-chan, Masaki, Kazu, Alice, Baron, Arthur, Judy, Kyoko, Hiro, Maya, Hicky, Macky, Darapi, Kimu, Nobby, Jusmin, Fumio, Jun, Toshi, Lily, Happy, Jin, Morimasa, Luke, Massa, Aya, Maya, Aga, Teruhi, Keiji, Naoko, Mina, Keiko, Itteki, Yumiko, Natsuki, Sumito, Ogu, Yoko, Tai, Gon, Chie, Takegon, Yoshiko, Massa, and Ayaka.

And last but not least, I'd like to thank my family: Masanobu, Kimiko, Isao, Michiko, Hiroko, Hiroyuki, Masamichi, Chiho, Momoka, Yasuhiro, Yumi, and most especially my wife, Julia, and daughter, Hana, who are the inspiration and joy of my life.

References

Attwood, J. B. *Maro Up!: The Secret to Success Begins with Arigato*. Amazon.com, 2012.

Dunn, E., and M. Norton. *Happy Money: The Science of Happier Spending*. New York: Simon & Schuster, 2014.

Honda, K. *8 Steps to Happiness and Prosperity (Shiawase-na Koganemochi)*. Tokyo: Goma Books, 2013.

———. *Money IQ and Money EQ (Okane no IQ, Okane no EQ)*. Tokyo: Goma Books, 2013.

Jampolsky, G. G. *Love Is Letting Go of Fear*. Random House Digital, 2011.

Luft, G., and A. Korin. *Turning Oil into Salt: Energy Independence Through Fuel Choice*. CreateSpace, 2009.

Scheinfeld, R. *Busting Loose from the Money Game: Mind-Blowing Strategies for Changing the Rules of a Game You Can't Win*. Hoboken, NJ: John Wiley, 2006.

Twist, L. *The Soul of Money: Transforming Your Relationship with Money and Life*. New York: W. W. Norton, 2006.